Graceful Beginnings
Short and Easy for Anyone New to the Bible

Satisfied by His Love

Let Jesus satisfy your heart with the goodness of His love

(Women Who Knew Jesus)

MELANIE NEWTON

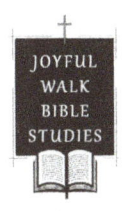

JOYFUL WALK BIBLE STUDIES

We express our thanks to those who served as editors for this study: Nancy Stephenson, Aimee Jones, Diane Bohannan, Linda Belmont, Jessica Power, Patty Cooke, and Elena Johnson.

© 2020 Melanie Newton. Published by Joyful Walk Press.

ISBN: 978-0-9978703-6-7

All rights reserved. Permission is granted to reproduce for personal and group use but not for resale. For questions about the use of this study guide, please visit melanienewton.com to contact us.

Cover graphic adapted from "bleeding-heart-bloom.jpg," a public domain online image.

> *All Scripture quotations, unless otherwise indicated, are taken from the Holy Bible, New International Version®, NIV®. Copyright ©1973, 1978, 1984, 2011 by Biblica, Inc.™ Used by permission of Zondervan. All rights reserved worldwide. www.zondervan.com The "NIV" and "New International Version" are trademarks registered in the United States Patent and Trademark Office by Biblica, Inc.™*

Melanie Newton is the author of "Graceful Beginnings" books for anyone new to the Bible and "Joyful Walk Bible Studies" for established Christians. Her mission is to help women learn to study the Bible for themselves and to grow their Bible-teaching skills to lead others. For questions about the use of this study guide, please visit melanienewton.com to contact us.

Joyful Walk Bible Studies are grace-based studies for women of all ages. Each study guide follows the inductive method of Bible study (observation, interpretation, application) in a warm and inviting format. We pray that you will find *Satisfied by His Love* to be a resource that God will use to strengthen you in your faith walk with Him.

JOYFUL WALK PRESS
Flower Mound, TX

MELANIE NEWTON

Melanie Newton is a Louisiana girl who made the choice to follow Jesus while attending LSU. She and her husband Ron married and moved to Texas for him to attend Dallas Theological Seminary. They stayed in Texas where Ron led a wilderness camping ministry for troubled youth for many years. Ron now helps corporations with their challenging employees and is the author of the top-rated business book, *No Jerks on the Job*.

Melanie jumped into raising three Texas-born children and serving in ministry to women at her church. Through the years, the Lord has given her opportunity to do Bible teaching and to write grace-based Bible studies for women that are now available from her website (melanienewton.com) and on Bible.org. *Graceful Beginnings* books are for anyone new to the Bible. *Joyful Walk Bible Studies* are for maturing Christians.

Melanie Newton loves to help women learn how to study the Bible for themselves. She also teaches online courses for women to grow their Bible-teaching skills to help others—all with the goal of getting to know Jesus more along the way. Her heart's desire is to encourage you to have a joyful relationship with Jesus Christ so you are willing to share that experience with others around you.

> "Jesus took hold of me in 1972, and I've been on this great adventure ever since. My life is a gift of God, full of blessings in the midst of difficult challenges. The more I've learned and experienced God's absolutely amazing grace, the more I've discovered my faith walk to be a joyful one. I'm still seeking that joyful walk every day…"

Melanie

OTHER BIBLE STUDIES BY MELANIE NEWTON

Graceful Beginnings Series books for anyone new to the Bible:

A Fresh Start: Beginning study for new Christians
Painting the Portrait of Jesus: A study of the Gospel of John
The God You Can Know: The character of our Father God
Grace Overflowing: A survey of Paul's letters
Satisfied by His Love: New Testament women
The Walk from Fear to Faith: Old Testament women
Seek the Treasure: Ephesians

Joyful Walk Bible Studies for growing Christians:

Graceful Living: The essentials of a grace-based Christian life
Everyday Women, Ever Faithful God: Old Testament women
Live Out His Love: New Testament women
Heartbreak to Hope: Good news from Mark
Radical Acts: Adventure with the Spirit from the book of Acts
The God-Dependent Woman: Life choices from 2 Corinthians
Knowing Jesus, Knowing Joy: A study of Philippians
Healthy Living: A study of Colossians
Perspective: A study of 1 and 2 Thessalonians
Adorn Yourself with Godliness: A study of 1 Timothy and Titus
To Be Found Faithful: A study of 2 Timothy
Profiles of Perseverance: Old Testament men
Reboot, Renew, Rejoice: A study of 1 and 2 Chronicles
Connecting Faith to Life on Planet Earth: A study of Genesis 1-11
Graceful Living Today: A 150-day devotional

Bible Study Leadership Courses

Bible Study Leadership Made Easy: online course
The 5 C's of Small Group Leadership: Handbook for leaders

Find these and more resources for your spiritual growth at joyfulwalkministries.org.

Contents

Introduction 1

A Woman Needing COMPASSION 7

A Woman Needing TRUTH 19

A Woman Needing FORGIVENESS 33

Two Women Needing HOPE 45

A Woman Needing FREEDOM 59

Two Women Needing ASSURANCE OF LOVE 73

Preview of "Seek the Treasure" 87

Sources 95

Introduction

GRACEFUL BEGINNINGS

The *Graceful Beginnings* books are Bible studies specifically designed for anyone new to the Bible—whether you are a new Christian or you just feel insecure about understanding the Bible. The short and easy lessons will introduce you to your God and His way of approaching life in simple terms that can be easily understood.

Just as a newborn baby needs to know the love and trustworthiness of her parents, the new Christian needs to know and experience the love and trustworthiness of her God. *A Fresh Start* is the first book in the series, laying a good foundation of truth for you to grasp and apply to your life. The other books in the series can be done in any order.

SOME BIBLE BASICS

Throughout these lessons, you will use a Bible to answer questions as you discover treasure about your life with Christ. The Bible is one book containing a collection of 66 books combined together for our benefit. It is divided into two main parts: Old Testament and New Testament.

The Old Testament tells the story of the beginning of the world and God's promises to mankind given through the nation of Israel. It tells how the people of Israel obeyed and disobeyed God over many, many years. All the stories and messages in the Old Testament lead up to Jesus Christ's coming to the earth.

The New Testament tells the story of Jesus Christ, the early Christians, and God's promises to all those who believe in Jesus. You can think of the Old Testament as "before Christ" and the New Testament as "after Christ."

Each book of the Bible is divided into chapters and verses within those chapters to make it easier to study. Bible references include the book name, chapter number and verse number(s). For example, Ephesians 2:8 refers to the New Testament book of Ephesians, the 2nd chapter, and verse 8 within that 2nd chapter. Printed Bibles have a "Table of Contents" in the front to help you locate books by page number. Bible apps also have a contents list by book and chapter.

The Bible verses highlighted at the beginning of each lesson in this study are from the New International Version® (NIV®) unless otherwise indicated. You can use any version of the Bible to answer the questions, but using a more easy-to-read translation (NIRV, NLT, NET, ESV) will help you gain confidence in understanding what you are reading. You can find all these translations in the "YouVersion App" or on biblegateway.com.

This study capitalizes certain pronouns referring to God, Jesus and the Holy Spirit—He, Him, His, Himself—just to make the reading of the study information less confusing. Some Bible translations likewise capitalize those pronouns referring to God; others do not. It is simply a matter of preference, not a requirement.

NEW TESTAMENT SUMMARY

The New Testament opens with the births of John the Baptist and Jesus. About 30 years later, John challenged the Jews to indicate their repentance (turning from sin and toward God) by submitting to water baptism—a familiar Old Testament practice used for repentance as well as when a non-Jew (often called Gentiles) converted to Judaism (to be washed clean of idolatry).

Jesus, who is also known by the title "Christ," is God's Son, fully God and fully man. Jesus publicly showed the world what God is like and taught His perfect ways for 3 – 3½ years. After preparing 12 disciples to continue Christ's earthly work, He died voluntarily on a cross for mankind's sin, rose from the dead, and returned to Heaven. The account of His earthly life is recorded in 4 books known as the Gospels (the biblical books of Matthew, Mark, Luke and John named after the compiler of each account).

After Jesus' return to Heaven, the followers of Christ were then empowered by the Holy Spirit and spread God's salvation message among the Jews, a number of whom believed in Christ. The apostle Paul and others carried the good news to the Gentiles during 3 missionary journeys (much of this recorded in the book of Acts). Paul wrote 13 New Testament letters to churches & individuals (Romans through Philemon). The section in our Bible from Hebrews to Jude contains 8 additional letters penned by five men, including two apostles (Peter and John) and two of Jesus' half-brothers (James and Jude, whose mother was Mary). The author of Hebrews is unknown. The apostle John also recorded Revelation, which summarizes God's final program for the world. The Bible ends as it began—with a new, sinless creation.

RELIGIOUS LEADERS IN JESUS' DAY

The **Pharisees** were a religious society of ~6,000 men who strictly obeyed the law of God as interpreted by the teachers of the law (also called scribes). This law consisted of the written Mosaic Law (found in the first five books of the Old Testament) plus the tradition of the elders (the oral law), containing hundreds of rules and prohibitions that were equally important to God's Law. They considered themselves to be Israel's spiritual leaders.

The **scribes**, also called lawyers or teachers of the Law, were an upper-class group of learned Jews who thoroughly knew and, therefore, interpreted the Mosaic Law. They were associated with the Pharisees. Many of them taught in the local seminary in Jerusalem. According to the tradition of the scribes, there were "secrets" of interpretation that they did not share with the common people thinking that God intended to leave the mass of people ignorant of His reasons for requiring certain things under the Law.

The **Sadducees** came from the leading families of Israel (e.g., the priests, merchants and aristocrats). The high priests and most powerful members of the priesthood were mainly Sadducees. The Sadducees rejected the tradition of the elders and did not believe in angels or miracles. They tended to be more upper class as comfortable compromisers with the Roman rulers. It has been estimated that in Jerusalem alone there were more than 20,000 associated with the Sadducees. Pharisees, by contrast, were middle class and more religious than the Sadducees.

The **Chief Priests** usually came from the class of Sadducees. This group included all the temple officers, including the High Priest and the captain of the temple.

Representatives from all these groups sat on the **Sanhedrin**, a religious governing body of 71 Jewish elders. They were elected, and then ordained by the laying on of hands. Their responsibilities included governing the Jewish community in religious matters related to the Law.

ELEMENTS OF EACH LESSON

This book covers the lives of several New Testament women. And, to help them seem more like real women, I suggest names in the lessons for those who are nameless. ☺

Each lesson begins with a Bible verse that relates to the focus of the lesson and a prayer. Prayer is just talking to God as conversation with someone who loves you dearly. The beginning prayer simply asks Jesus to teach you through the lesson. This is followed by a brief description of the cultural influences that affected the lives of the women who lived then.

Work through each lesson, reading the scripture passages that tell each woman's "Story." You'll be encouraged at the end of each lesson to write something about your own faith experience that relates to what's learned in the lesson. Your faith walk is your story, your biography of God's faithfulness to you and your response back to Him.

A "Jesus Satisfies" teaching session follows each lesson and encourages your heart to be satisfied by an aspect of Jesus' love for you. You can listen to this as a podcast from melanienewton.com/podcasts. Look for *"2: Live Out His Love, Satisfied by His Love"* to find the one for each lesson. You can also find these podcasts on most podcast providers.

Every "Jesus Satisfies" section is followed by a "Reflect" time for you to respond to what you learned and a prayer of trust that Jesus will satisfy your heart through knowing Him.

There is also a suggested reading through the gospel of Luke, 4 chapters per week, with space for you to reflect on what you just read.

SMALL GROUP DISCUSSION

While you can work through these lessons as a personal study, this topic is perfect to use for small groups. Share the following suggested guidelines with the group members to maximize your discussion group experience.

- Set aside some time each week to do the study questions so that you will get to know God better.
- Consistently attend whether your lesson is done or not. You will learn from the discussion.
- Respect each other's insights. Listen thoughtfully. Share your own insights, but do not dominate the discussion.
- Celebrate unity in Christ by avoiding controversial subjects such as politics, divisive issues and denominational differences.
- Maintain confidentiality of whatever is shared within the group.

Enjoy your small group discussion and learn from one another. As you share parts of your story with your group members, you will have a greater connection with each other. And, you'll have more reason to praise our ever-faithful God as you see and hear how He has been faithful to each of you through the years. A small group is a great place to share how you are "Satisfied by His Love." Discussing the lesson and the teaching session should take about an hour, making this an easy study to fit into a busy workday schedule.

Suggested Leader Guide for Group Discussion:

1. Pray for the Holy Spirit to teach you what He wants you to know through the lesson.
2. Work through the lesson together, reading the Bible verses and discussing the questions. Predetermine which of the explanatory paragraphs you will read as a group.
3. Read the "SATISFIED BY HIS LOVE" summary paragraph and share responses to the application question that follows.
5. Discuss parts of the "JESUS SATISFIES" section that you want to emphasize. REFLECT on the teaching.
6. Pray for the group members – ask Jesus to satisfy your hearts through knowing Him. Thank God for His grace toward you and His love for you.
7. Remind each person to do the next lesson and listen to the related podcast before the group meets again.

SATISFIED BY HIS LOVE

The Lord Jesus demonstrated in His life on earth how much He loved and valued women. He showed them compassion, taught them truth, forgave their sins, freed them from bondage, gave them hope through dire situations, and assured them of His love for them. Because His care for them was so countercultural to what they had previously known, women responded with love for Him and a desire to serve Him. Many of them had walks of faith that brought challenges as well as times of joy. They focused on following Jesus and serving Him in their daily lives. Jesus Christ entered into the midst of their lives, visibly representing God to them, loving them dearly, and changing their lives forever! He does the same for you and me today.

My heart's desire is to encourage you through this study to have an authentic, loving relationship with Jesus Christ for yourself so that your heart is truly satisfied with good things by His love. Hopefully, you will then be willing to share that experience with others around you. Just relax, trust in Him, and begin an adventure that will transform your life and others as well. Are you ready for adventure? It's going to be a great journey. And, I'm so glad to be walking beside you!

Melanie Newton

Higher than the mountains that I face
Stronger than the power of the grave
Constant through the trial and the change
One thing remains, this one thing remains
Your love never fails, it never gives up;
It never runs out on me, Your love
Because on and on and on and on it goes
Before it overwhelms and **satisfies my soul**
And I never, ever, have to be afraid
One thing remains, this one thing remains
Your love never fails, it never gives up; it never runs out on me
Your love

(*One Thing Remains* by Jesus Culture)

1 A Woman Needing COMPASSION

"The LORD is compassionate and gracious, slow to anger, abounding in love." (PSALM 103:8)

Pray: Lord Jesus, please teach me through this lesson.

THE NEED TO BE SATISFIED

A woman's greatest felt need is to have her heart's desires satisfied by love, security, and significance.

The quest for satisfaction became the driving force behind women of the '80s and '90s. As women tuned into the highly mobile, high-tech society around them, they began to turn their energies to new frontiers. To excel, to succeed, even to surpass the accomplishments of their male counterparts, has been the goal of many women who have challenged men's domain.

Now, however, as women examine who they have become, many are wondering where they really belong. It has become painfully clear that achievement and success have not delivered the payoff of personal satisfaction that women seek. In the brief reflective spaces sandwiched between their frenzied commitments, women are now realizing that external accomplishments do not satisfy their deepest inner longings. So, the search for satisfaction continues.

What many don't realize is that each woman is created by God with a built-in spiritual need for a relationship with Him. This spiritual hunger and thirst is as real as physical hunger and thirst. The way to have it satisfied is just as real though not always obvious. Yet, the desire to satisfy this hunger and thirst draws women toward the spiritual arena. I was that woman in 1972 when I was invited to join a small women's Bible study group at college. There, I met Jesus in the pages of the Bible. As my relationship grew with Him, I recognized a deep sense of being satisfied. My longing to know God was being fulfilled. It still is.

Regardless of your age or stage of life, circumstances or personality, you were created with a built-in spiritual hunger that only God can satisfy. God sent His Son Jesus to live as a man and die for your sins so that you can have your deepest needs satisfied just by knowing Him. To get there, you need to know the answers to these questions, "Who is Jesus Christ, and why did He come?" You also need the answer to "How did He treat women, and can I as a woman know Him today?" Perhaps you are the one thinking, "Why don't I feel satisfied in my life? How can I get my deepest needs and longings satisfied?"

Today begins your journey to answer those questions. Let's start here:

> *What have you tried to satisfy your built-in spiritual thirst apart from Christ? (It's okay to say, "I don't know.)*

> *How did that work for you?*

THE GOD WHO SATISFIES

Read Psalm 107:4-9. (The book of Psalms is in the Old Testament.)

The writer of this psalm (a prayer or song) describes those who are wandering, seeking something to satisfy their hunger and thirst.

> *What are the wanderers experiencing (verses 4-5)?*

> *When they cry out to the Lord (verse 6), what does He do for them (verses 7 and 9)?*

If our God created us with a spiritual thirst for a relationship with Him (as the Bible declares), a relationship with another human cannot satisfy that thirst. Only God can satisfy the thirsty heart.

His plan to do that included coming to earth to take on a human body and to live as a man among us. Enter Jesus. As the radical rabbi, Jesus treated women as no man had ever treated them before. His warmth, personal attention, tenderness, sound teaching, and compassion toward women were revolutionary. He openly demonstrated His love for each individual He met—both men and women—for whom He would ultimately die. A relationship with Jesus satisfies every person's built-in spiritual thirst.

CONNECTING WITH NEW TESTAMENT WOMEN

To fully appreciate Jesus' approach to women, we need to resist our impulse to approach the Bible from our twenty-first century cultural perspective. Our understanding is more accurate if we step back in time—into the shoes of the women of the first century AD.

It was tough to be a woman living around the rim of the Mediterranean during Jesus' time. In both Greek and Roman cultures, women held a second-rate status. Their legal rights were few, and women were generally treated like property. Jewish women fared slightly better than their contemporaries in surrounding cultures.

You may have limited knowledge of the New Testament so these women may be strangers to you. When you read the gospels, you can easily think, "What's written in it happened so long ago! What do those women have in common with **me**? They didn't live in **my** world." Yet, they were still women like you and I are.

As everyday women, they cooked meals, did laundry, and raised children. They had responsibilities inside and outside of their homes. They experienced hormone fluctuations and menopause. They laughed with their friends, differed with their mates, and cried when a loved one died. I bet they all found ways to use their 20,000 words per day. ☺

At one time, they were 20-somethings, then 40-somethings, then 60-somethings and more. They wore beads, earrings, and ankle bracelets. Their hair needed to be combed and fixed, and it turned grey as they aged. No doubt, some of them, if not all, had something on their bodies that sagged!

These women also experienced fear at various times just like we do. They faced rejection from peers, sick family members, and disappointments. They faced trauma and surprise houseguests. They even had "bad" days when things didn't go right, sometimes due to their own choices. These were everyday women, just like we are.

> *As women, what kinds of life experiences for them might have been the same as your own?*

> *What kinds of deep longings did these women have that you may also experience?*

Their stories—snippets of their biographies—are preserved for us to get to know them and to know their Savior who is also our Savior. Jesus is the ever-faithful Son of God whose character never changes and who acts on our behalf to satisfy every hunger and thirst that we have. One of His character qualities that is evident as He acts on our behalf is compassion. Every woman needs compassion from Jesus, whether she knows it or not.

A Woman's Need for Compassion

> "Compassion is understanding the troubles of others, coupled with an urgent desire to help...Compassion is a heart's response to a person's need combined with a helping hand that offers mercy and grace." (Carol Kent, *Becoming a Woman of Influence*, p. 109, 111)

Compassion is not just feeling. It is doing something to ease someone's pain, whether it's for this week or more. Compassion is proactive. Psalm 103:8 says, "The Lord is compassionate and gracious."

> *When do you need the Lord's compassion?*

Jesus embodied God's compassion to those He met. The gospels record many incidents of Jesus expressing compassion towards people. Let's look at just a few of them.

Read Matthew 14:14.

For whom did Jesus feel compassion, and what did He do?

Read Matthew 15:32-37.

For whom did Jesus feel compassion, and what did He do?

Read Mark 6:34.

For whom did Jesus feel compassion, and what did He do?

Let's look at the life of one woman who certainly needed the compassion of Jesus. Since she is from Nain, we will call her 'Nancy.'

A little bit of history

In the Jewish culture, great celebration occurred at the birth of a son. Providing a son gave a woman value in her husband's eyes as the son ensured that the family wealth and name would continue to the next generation. It would also be his responsibility to care for his aging parents, and especially his mother once widowed. Having a son was the hope of every Jewish woman. Jesus was well into His ministry when He met such a woman.

After healing a Roman centurion's servant, Jesus and His disciples headed to a city called Nain, about 10 miles southeast of Jesus' hometown of Nazareth. As He entered Nain, a funeral procession for a "young man" (18-30 years old) was leaving town. Funerals were often held the same day as the death because of the heat and lack of embalming. Bystanders were obligated to follow a funeral procession, with hired mourners adding to the wails of friends. The body was wrapped in cloth and carried on a stretcher. After the funeral, mourning continued for 30 days.

Read Luke 7:11-17.

If you have experienced the death of someone very close to you, you probably understand the widow's state of mind when she encountered Jesus.

> *Put yourself in 'Nancy's' place, what could she have been feeling and thinking when Jesus first saw her?*

> *According to verse 13, when Jesus saw her, what did He feel and say to 'Nancy'?*

> *What happened next?*
> - Verse 14—
>
> - Verse 15—

> *Put yourself in 'Nancy's' place, what could she have been feeling and thinking after her son was restored to her?*

What other lives were impacted by Jesus' compassion on 'Nancy' (verses 16-17)?

Jesus could have just passed by and assumed the town would meet 'Nancy's' basic needs of food and shelter. But, He didn't.

When Jesus said not to cry, He wasn't being mean or saying that crying is wrong. He was telling her she could stop because He was going to heal her hurt. Jesus had *compassion* on her and took action to relieve the suffering. Jesus represented His Father's heart for people. And, Jesus' encounter with 'Nancy' and her son ended up touching many lives.

SATISFIED BY HIS LOVE

When Jesus entered Nain, He saw a woman who was obviously a widow walking next to her dead son in a coffin. He knew this was her only son. He knew and understood her deep hurt and fear about what would happen to her. His heart went out to her, and He compassionately gave her son back to her. When Jesus said goodbye to 'Nancy,' He left a woman who no doubt felt satisfied by His love and compassion for her.

Isn't it comforting to know that when you are in pain, God's heart goes out to you? He feels your pain. He cares for you. He comforts you. He acts on your behalf. He is not a cold, distant, helpless Deity but is a loving, compassionate God.

The verse you read at the beginning of this lesson, Psalm 103:8, says that God crowns you with compassion. To be crowned with compassion means to be surrounded with it so that you have a sense of God's favor and protection. The widow had that.

Jesus personally invites you to bring your deepest longings, heartaches, and anxieties to Him today, just as men and women did in the ancient past.

Are you confident that you can go to Him and openly express your deepest needs? Often, Jesus responds by giving you a Bible verse to grasp. Or, He sends someone to alleviate your suffering through bringing a meal, visiting, calling, providing clothes, or just listening and giving counsel and prayer.

> Christians often do not know what to say to someone who is grieving, or they say things that hurt more than help (for example, "You can have another child" or "She's in a better place"). One of the nicest things someone wrote to me in a card after my father died several years ago was this, "Knowing you, I look forward to meeting your dad in Heaven one day." I cherish that card. *Melanie*
>
> **What hurts do you have today? Talk to Jesus and tell Him about your hurts, knowing He has compassion for you.**

JESUS SATISFIES YOUR HEART WITH COMPASSION

Recommended: Listen to the podcast *"New Testament Women Learn How Jesus Satisfies Our Hearts"*. *Use the following as a listener guide.*

To fully appreciate Jesus' approach to women, we need to step back in time—into the shoes of the women of the first century AD.

It was tough to be a woman living around the rim of the Mediterranean during Jesus' time. In both Greek and Roman cultures, women held a second-rate status with few legal rights.

Jewish women fared better than their Roman contemporaries. Married women with children held a place of honor as wife and mother, but even that position was tied to her ability to produce male children. In an agricultural society, fathers needed sons (lots of them) to help them work the land. At the birth of a son, all celebrated. Not so much at the birth of a daughter.

Jesus—the one who wants us

Jesus Christ entered into the midst of this culture with a radically different value system from that of His culture in the way He regarded women. His compassion for women elevated their position in society and gave them equal relationship with Him. Reading through the gospels, you can see that...

- ➤ He spoke to women publicly when a rabbi wouldn't speak publicly to his wife.
- ➤ He let them travel with Him during His public ministry and support Him with their own money.
- ➤ He taught women openly and continually when the rabbis didn't consider them able to be educated.
- ➤ He defended them when they were criticized.
- ➤ He was sensitive and compassionate toward women and healed their loved ones.

> He made them the first witnesses to His resurrection when women were considered to be unreliable as witnesses.

Jesus never spoke condescendingly to women, made derogatory jokes about women, or humiliated women. And women who knew Him loved Him, wanting to follow and serve Him!

Jesus treated women as no man had ever treated them before. His warmth, personal attention, tenderness, sound teaching, and compassion toward women were revolutionary. And why shouldn't He be compassionate toward women? Jesus is fully God, and He created us!

Jesus—the one who understands us

He was there in the beginning when God said, "Let us make mankind in our image, in our likeness…" (Genesis 1:26).

As Creator, **He designed us with a mind to know God, emotions to love God, and a will to obey God**. Our female minds need to be filled with the knowledge of Him so that our hearts may respond with great love for Him and so that our wills can choose to obey Him.

Jesus knows us backwards and forwards—our emotional nature, our need for security and significance, and even our hormones! He understands our need to nurture and to be loved—both from those humans closest to us and from our Creator God. And even though His culture neglected to give women the worth they deserved, He could do no less than show that He loves men and women equally—for whom He would ultimately die.

Here's a key truth I want you to grasp. *A relationship with Jesus satisfies every spiritual need that you and I have. Every one of them. You don't need to go anywhere else to get those deep needs satisfied.*

Jesus—the one who meets our needs

The writer of Psalm 103 lists benefits that you may receive from God as He meets your needs. Let's look at them.

> *"Praise the Lord, my soul, and forget not all His benefits—who forgives all your sins and heals all your diseases, who redeems your life from the pit and crowns you with love and compassion, who **satisfies your desires with good things** so that your youth is renewed like the eagle's." (Psalm 103:2-5)*

Do you need forgiveness? Jesus does that. Do you need healing and hope for dire circumstances? Jesus does that. Are you in bondage to something? Jesus frees you from bondage. Do you need assurance that you are loved? Jesus crowns you with His love and compassion. To be crowned with compassion means to be surrounded with it so that you have a sense of God's favor and protection. The widow had that. You can, too.

Our God promises to satisfy your heart's desires with good things. You will be so satisfied that you will feel renewed and released to soar like an eagle. Have you watched an eagle soar on an updraft of air? You and I can soar as our God lifts us up from the pit where our souls are so hungry and thirsty, and He fills us with everything we need to feel satisfied. Satisfied by His love.

Jesus' heart went out to this grieving widow. Isn't it comforting to know that when you are in pain, God's heart goes out to you? He feels your pain. He cares for you. He comforts you. He acts on your behalf. He is not a cold, distant, helpless Deity but is a loving, compassionate God. Jesus personally invites you to bring your deepest longings, heartaches, and anxieties to Him today, just as men and women did in the ancient past. He wants to satisfy your heart needs.

Our God created us with a spiritual thirst for a relationship with Him. A relationship with another human cannot satisfy that thirst. Only God can satisfy the thirsty heart. As the Bible promises,

> *"for He satisfies the thirsty and fills the hungry with good things." (Psalm 107:9)*

A satisfied heart senses God's favor and compassion.

Let Jesus satisfy your heart with the goodness of His love.

REFLECT

> **When you did go to Him and tell Him about your pain or needing help, what did He do for you? How did He show His compassion for you?**

> *Pray: Ask Jesus to satisfy your heart through knowing Him. Trust Him to work in your life to bring you healing, hope, and freedom. Thank Him for His grace toward you and His unending love for you.*

Deeper Discoveries: Read Luke chapters 1-4. Reflect on what you read.

Luke 1—

Luke 2—

Luke 3—

Luke 4—

10-28-21

❤ 2 A Woman Needing TRUTH

"Jesus answered, 'I am the way and the truth and the life. No one comes to the Father except through me.'" (John 14:6)

> Pray: Lord Jesus, please teach me through this lesson.

A Little Bit of History

In Jesus' time, the two main geographical areas of the country of Israel were Galilee to the north and Judea to the south. Jerusalem, the capital city of Israel, was located in the south. Nazareth, Cana, Capernaum and other cities where Jesus spent most of His time were located in Galilee. Between those two areas was the territory called Samaria, home of the Samaritans.

The Samaritans were considered to be half-breeds, the product of mixed marriages between Jews and the foreign people imported by Assyria (a country that spanned modern-day Syria and northern Iraq) when it conquered the northern Kingdom in 722 BC. The Samaritans had a polluted worship of God, insisting God should be worshiped on their Mount Gerizim. The Samaritan Bible contained only the books of Moses (Genesis through Deuteronomy) so they knew very little of God apart from that.

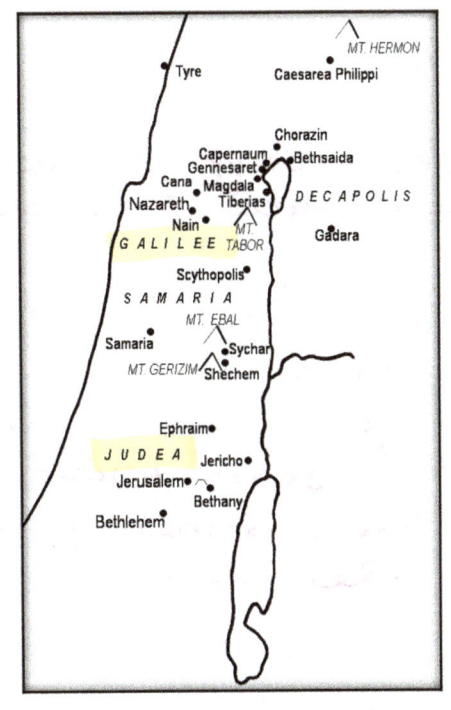

A WOMAN NEEDING TRUTH   19

The Jews hated the Samaritans. Just being near them would make a Jew feel dirty. Though going through Samaria was the shortest route from Judea to Galilee, the Jews normally crossed the Jordan River to travel on the east side in order to avoid Samaria, especially since the Samaritans were generally hostile to traveling Jews. Jesus, however, was not the typical Jew. Nothing could make him unclean. He travels through Samaria, and there He meets and talks with a Samaritan woman. Let's call her 'Samantha.'

Read John 2:25.

What does Jesus know?

Jesus knows whats in a man's heart.

Read John 4:4-15.

What did Jesus do when He got to Sychar (verses 5-6)?

Jesus stopped @ Jacob's well as He was tired from the journey.

Jesus was fully God and fully man. As a man, He experienced thirst, weariness, pain, and hunger. The "sixth hour" was noon according to Roman time.

How did Jesus begin a relationship with 'Samantha' (verse 7)?

Jesus asked the woman for a drink of water from the well.

'Samantha' recognized Jesus as a Jew so she questioned His even talking to her. What gift did Jesus offer her in verse 10?

living water — eternal life.

What additional explanation about "living water" does Jesus give to her in verses 13-14?

"Whoever drinks the water Jesus gives will never thirst. And the water Jesus gives is eternal life."

How did 'Samantha' respond (verse 15)?

She didn't understand Jesus was offering spiritual life — eternal life.

Read John 7:37-39.

When Jesus told her about "living water" (John 4:14), what was He offering to her?

spiritual life = eternal life

Normally, a Jewish man would not speak publicly to women. But, Jesus did not hesitate to start the conversation. Drawing water was a daily chore for women. 'Samantha' thought Jesus was offering a way to meet that need to get water without her having to work for it. To the people of Jesus' day, "living water" referred to flowing water from a stream or spring rather than the still water found in a well or cistern. Such "living water" was highly valued. "Living water" in the Bible also referred to spiritual life. Jesus was offering to satisfy a deeper need than just physical thirst—the need for spiritual life, which is given by the Holy Spirit.

Read John 4:16-26.

In verses 16-18, what does Jesus know about her that shows you He is also God? (See John 2:25.)

Jesus knew that she currently had no husband but previously had 5 husbands. And the man she was living with now was not her husband.

This time, what need(s) do you think He was addressing in 'Samantha's' life?

how she is searching for love with different husbands.

Jesus gets to meddling in her personal life, pointing out an area of need she can't meet on her own—to have real love, a moral life, and fulfilling relationships. In a few words, Jesus revealed her sin and her need for salvation. It's as though He was asking, "How's that working for you?"

How does 'Samantha' change the subject in verses 19-20?

Samaritans worshipped on this mountain but Jesus claim Jerusalem is where they must worship.

What truth does Jesus say about worship in the following verses?

- Verse 21— *a time is coming when you will worship neither on this mountain nor in Jerusalem.*
- Verse 22— *Samaritans worship what they do not know. Jews worship what they do know. Salvation is from the Jews.*
- Verses 23-24— *God is spirit & His worshippers must worship Him in spirit & in truth. These are the kind of worshipers the Father seeks*

'Samantha' diverts the conversation away from her personal life to a controversial issue about where to worship God. Jesus responds by giving her truth (twice He mentions "truth")—true worship is not dependent on a place but on "spirit and truth." The term "spirit" probably refers to the Holy Spirit of God who dwells inside all Christians and guides every believer to do what pleases God. True worship of God will be directed by the presence of the Holy Spirit and be rooted in the truth (meaning all of God's written revelation, not just the books of Moses). Notice that 'Samantha' refers to "our fathers" (verse 20) referring to traditions she knew. <mark>Jesus introduces God as **"the Father,"** indicating someone with whom she can have a loving relationship</mark> (verse 23). This is more truth to satisfy her spiritual thirst.

Once again, Samantha changes the subject. What does she declare (verse 25)? She knows that the messiah is coming & then He will explain everything. to them.

What truth does Jesus give to her about Himself (verse 26)? Jesus declared "I who speak to you am He."

The title "Christ" is from the Greek word *christos,* a translation of the Hebrew term "Messiah" meaning "anointed one." The Old Testament prophets promised that the Messiah, as the anointed one of God, would come and do many wonderful things for God's people, including restoring God's Kingdom on earth. Christians are followers of Jesus, who is the Christ. 'Samantha' knew a little truth—a Messiah is coming. Jesus gave her more truth—He is that promised Messiah.

Read John 4:27-30.

How did 'Samantha' respond to Jesus and His conversation with her (verses 28-29)? She left her water jar & went back to the town & told the people "Come see a man who told me everything I ever did. Could this be the Christ?"

What did she leave behind (verse 28)?

her water jar

How did the townspeople respond to Samantha's news (verse 30)?

> They came out of the town & went to see Jesus.

Read John 4:39-42.

How did the townspeople respond to what they heard (verses 39-40)?

> Many Samaritans believed in Jesus because of the woman's testimony. They urged Jesus to stay.

How long did Jesus stay to teach the Samaritans truth?

> The people urged Jesus to stay w/ them — and He stayed 2 days.

What were the results (verse 41-42)?

> Because of Jesus' words many more became believers. They believed because they heard for themselves that Jesus is the Savior of the world.

'Samantha's' words to her neighbors raised curiosity among them as Jesus had done with her. They came to see for themselves, and many believed in Him because of her story. They offered hospitality, urging Him to stay and continue teaching them truth that they then believed. In the last lesson, you read this:

"When Jesus landed and saw a large crowd, He had compassion on them, because they were like sheep without a shepherd. So, He began teaching them many things." (Mark 6:34)

That is what Jesus is doing here—teaching truth to men and women who had been deprived of it before this.

Read John 6:40.

What is the Father's will? that everyone who believes in Jesus shall have eternal life & they will be raised up on the last day.

Read John 14:6.

What does Jesus declare about Himself? Jesus said "I am the way & the truth & the life. No one comes to the Father except thru me."

We can confidently say this: Jesus is the way to know God as the Father because Jesus shows us the truth about God in His life, and He gives His life to anyone who believes in Him. What about you today? Do you believe that Jesus is the way to know God as your Father?

SATISFIED BY HIS LOVE

'Samantha' grew up knowing only half-truths. And, because she was deficient in truth, she could not have a proper relationship with the true God. Her need for spiritual life remained unsatisfied. Then, Jesus entered her life. Jesus is the Son of God who came to live as a man on this earth and to give eternal life to anyone who would believe in Him.

'Samantha' needed this truth as did every other person Jesus met on earth. Jesus satisfied her need for real life, real love, and fulfilling relationships by giving her Himself. And, He continues to offer that to everyone today.

By knowing the truth about Jesus and experiencing a relationship with Him, you will also be satisfied by His love.

Think about your story of knowing Jesus and respond according to your own experience:

- If you have already trusted in Jesus to be your Savior, think back to what life was like before knowing Jesus. What triggered your need for Jesus? What did God use to draw you to Him?

- As a Christian, what have you done to stay faithful to Him through the years?

- If you have not made the decision to believe that Jesus is who He says He is—God's Son, you can put your trust in Him today and experience His love for you right away. If you do this, tell someone. If you are still unsure, ask Jesus to reveal Himself through the truth of His Word. Ask someone to meet with you and answer questions you might have.

Your response:

JESUS SATISFIES YOUR HEART WITH TRUTH

JESUS SATISFIES

Recommended: *Listen to the podcast "Samaritan Woman: Jesus Satisfies Your Heart with Truth." Use the following as a listener guide.*

On the night before His trial and crucifixion, Jesus told His disciples that He was going to heaven to prepare a place for them, and they could follow because they knew the way to get there.

But one of His disciples named Thomas wasn't so sure about this. So, Thomas asked Jesus, "How can we know the way?" Jesus answered with a strong declaration of truth,

> "'I am the way and the truth and the life. No one comes to the Father except through me." (John 14:6)

We can confidently say this: Jesus is the **way** to know God as Father because He shows us the **truth** about God in His life, and He gives His **life** to anyone who believes in Him.

Let's look at each one of those words—WAY, TRUTH, and LIFE.

Jesus is the WAY.

Jesus says He is the only way for any person to have a relationship with God the Heavenly Father by simply believing in Him.

Shortly after Jesus' resurrection and ascension back to Heaven, one of Jesus' followers named Peter confidently declared to the religious leaders of Jerusalem,

> "Salvation is found in no one else [but Jesus], for there is no other name under heaven given to mankind by which we must be saved." (Acts 4:12)

The first Christians were so convinced of Jesus being the only way to know God and taught this truth everywhere so they were called "followers of the way." As a "follower of the way," the apostle Paul traveled extensively preaching that Jesus is the way to know God, the way to receive forgiveness for your sins, and the way to live a life that pleases God. Anyone who asked him, "How can I know God?" Paul would answer, "Believe in the Lord Jesus Christ." He's the WAY.

Based on this understanding, would you identify yourself as a "follower of the way?"

Other people may try to tell you that there are many ways to get to Heaven, such as just being a good person or doing good works. Or, they might say there are other gods out there besides the God of the Bible.

But, you can tell them only one man died on the cross to pay the penalty for your sins: Jesus. Only one man was ever resurrected from the dead with a new body that will never die again: Jesus. Only Jesus was truly God. Anyone who believes in Jesus can now have forgiveness of their sins and a relationship with God.

No other religious leader has ever been resurrected from the dead, and they are all in their graves. Jesus is not in His grave. He was resurrected from the grave, given a new body, and is sitting in Heaven on His kingly throne ready to welcome you and me when we trust in Him.

Jesus is the only way for any person to have a relationship with God. You have to start with that and believe that. Jesus said He is the **way**. Jesus also said He is the truth.

Jesus is the TRUTH.

After Jesus told His disciples that He was the way, the truth, and the life, the next thing He said was very important.

> "If you really know me, you will know my Father as well. From now on, you do know Him and have seen Him." (John 14:7)

When Jesus was on earth, He showed everyone the truth about God the Father. Jesus was loving and kind, showing us God is loving and kind. Jesus was always good, showing us that God is always good. Jesus showed us that God answers prayer and that God hates sin. Jesus was the living truth of God.

Jesus declared this to a crowd listening to Him,

> "If you hold to my teaching, you are really my disciples. Then you will know the truth, and the **truth will set you free**." (John 8:31-32)

Knowing the truth will set you free from error, misconceptions, ad bondage to lies that have prevented you from having a satisfying relationship with God in your life.

Jesus was the truth of God back then and is still the truth of God. Truth never changes. Jesus is the truth. Jesus is also the life.

Jesus is the LIFE.

Anyone who believes in Jesus not only has a relationship with God but also receives eternal life. Eternal life starts the moment you believe in Jesus, can never end, and no one can take it away from you!

That is Jesus' promise to us when He said,

> "I am the resurrection and the life. The one who believes in me will live, even though they die...." (John 11:25)

Even though your body dies, your soul lives on in Heaven where you will one day receive a new body just like Jesus' new body, one that will never die again. That's eternal life. But, when Jesus said He is the life, He meant even more than that. Paul describes this beautifully in Galatians 2…

> "I have been crucified with Christ and I no longer live, but Christ lives in me. The life I now live in the body, I live by faith in the Son of God, who loved me and gave Himself for me." (Galatians 2:20)

As part of God's family, God's Spirit comes to live inside you and enables you to live a life that pleases God your Father. He changes the way you think and feel to be more like the way Jesus thought and felt when He was on earth. Jesus is the truth that satisfies.

Our God created us with a spiritual thirst for a relationship with Him. Another human cannot satisfy that thirst. Only God can satisfy the thirsty heart. As the Bible promises,

> "for He satisfies the thirsty and fills the hungry with good things." (Psalm 107:9)

A satisfied heart stands firmly on the truth that brings real life and real love and fulfilling relationships.

Let Jesus satisfy your heart with the goodness of His love.

Reflect

Read the following prayer and then express what it means to you to be satisfied by Jesus' life in you.

How absolutely amazing is your loving plan, oh God, that takes care of my need to know you! Help me to hold onto the truth that Jesus is the only way to have a relationship with God as my Father. Help me to believe that I am truly your child, completely loved and accepted by you the moment I trusted in Jesus. Fill my heart with joy and celebration because Jesus' life is inside me.

Pray: Ask Jesus to satisfy your heart through knowing Him. Trust Him to work in your life to bring you healing, hope, and freedom. Thank Him for His grace toward you and His unending love for you.

Deeper Discoveries: Read Luke chapters 5-8. Reflect on what you read.

Luke 5—

Luke 6—

Luke 7—

Luke 8—

3 A Woman Needing FORGIVENESS

"Therefore, I tell you, her many sins have been forgiven—for she loved much. But he who has been forgiven little loves little." (Luke 7:47)

> Pray: Lord Jesus, please teach me through this lesson.

A Little Bit of History

After Jesus' encounter with the Samaritan woman, He continued teaching and performing many miracles. It was a time of great popularity when Jesus gained many followers. He chose His 12 disciples and preached the Sermon on the Mount. He spent time traveling throughout Galilee and in the area of Capernaum (a sizeable town on the north shore of the Sea of Galilee). Peter (one of the 12 disciples) had a house there that became Jesus' base of operations during His extended ministry in Galilee. The inhabitants of Capernaum had many opportunities to see and hear Jesus and to offer hospitality to Him.

Hospitality to guests was one of the most important social functions of Jesus' time. A guest was highly honored even if he was a stranger passing through the town. When a stranger appeared at someone's door close to evening, the head of the household usually let him in and asked him to spend the night.

If the homeowner refused to be hospitable, he could be snubbed by friends and neighbors. A host always kept in mind that someday he, too, might be a weary traveler looking for shelter and company.

Once inside, the host's wife or servant brought water to wash the guest's feet, though the host might do it for a special guest. Since the roads were always dusty and most people walked, washing was a common courtesy that made one's guest feel at home. At mealtime, the guest would often be served first. Other customs included anointing the guest with oil, which they used as soap, or even providing clean clothing for the mealtime.

According to custom, a guest should stay no longer than three days in his host's home. While there, he was protected by his host. On leaving, the host was to escort his guest a short distance, sending him safely on his way.

One day, Jesus was a guest in someone's home...

Read Luke 7:36-50.

The Pharisees were a religious society of ~6,000 men who strictly obeyed the Jewish laws as interpreted by the teachers of the law (also called scribes). This law consisted of the written Mosaic Law (found in the first five books of the Old Testament) plus the tradition of the elders, containing hundreds of rules and prohibitions that they thought were equally important to God's Law. They considered themselves to be Israel's spiritual leaders.

Though originally standing against evil in Jewish society, by Jesus' day many Pharisees had become narrow-minded and petty, more concerned with rules than with relationships, even with God. They looked at other Jews as well as Gentiles (anyone who was not a Jew) as tainted and, therefore, to be avoided. In their minds, no rabbi (Jewish "pastor") or religious leader should mingle or eat with such "sinners." Jesus confronted this wrong view of people. So, many Pharisees were opposed to Him.

> *Simon the Pharisee invited Jesus to dinner. What did he call Jesus in verse 40?*

Jesus accepted an invitation to dinner from a Pharisee. He did not cut all the religious leaders off simply because most of them rejected Him. He dealt with people as individuals, and He still does!

The men are reclining around a table as they eat. A woman enters the scene. Let's call her 'Emma.'

Who is 'Emma' (verse 37)?

What does she do (verses 37-38)?

Put yourself in 'Emma's' place. Why do you think she was weeping as she poured perfume on Jesus' feet?

Both the alabaster jar and the perfume inside were very costly and could have been 'Emma's' dowry or her savings. What was she giving to Jesus?

If you are thinking that this woman "crashed the party," social custom allowed needy people to visit such meals and to partake of some of the leftovers. And, it was not unusual for people to drop in when a rabbi was visiting. 'Emma' must have heard Jesus teach, which might have given her hope for a new life. Overcome by her brokenness and her need for forgiveness, 'Emma' gave to Him the most precious thing she had.

What was Simon the Pharisee thinking while this was happening (verse 39)?

Jesus read his thoughts (only God can do that) and took the opportunity to teach Simon. What does Jesus teach through the parable (verses 40-43)?

Then, how does Jesus address Simon's harsh attitude in verses 44-47?

Simon viewed this heartbroken woman as dirty and someone to be avoided. Jesus read his thoughts showing that He was indeed a prophet. Remember John 2:25 from Lesson Two? Jesus always knows what is in the heart of men and women.

Jesus contrasted Simon's lack of courtesy and respect for Him as a guest with the woman's tender attentions to Him. The Pharisees didn't recognize their own need for forgiveness because they "followed" the rules, yet their hearts were hard toward God and people. I heard someone say that your capacity to love is directly tied to your capacity to get how deeply you have been forgiven. When you see yourself as righteous and not needing anything from Jesus (like Simon), you lose compassion for the lost and needy. 'Emma' knew how deeply she needed forgiveness.

In verses 47-48, what does Jesus grant to 'Emma'?

What else does He say to her in verse 50?

Put yourself in 'Emma's' shoes. She needed something from Jesus. For what need(s) do you think she came to Him?

What did Jesus give to her to satisfy those needs so that she could choose a different kind of life?

Jesus grants forgiveness and peace to 'Emma' because of her faith and love. She needed a relationship with God, forgiveness for her sins, and a chance for a new life. He accepted her gift of love and publicly acknowledged her faith and forgiveness. Jesus gave her respect, hope, and a new beginning. 'Emma' could go in peace with her need for forgiveness completely satisfied by Jesus' love for her. She now has to make choices to live a different kind of life and hopefully leave her life of immorality.

SATISFIED BY HIS LOVE

Jesus took notice of this "worthless" woman of the town. Because she was held in bondage by her sin, she could not have a proper relationship with the true God. Her need for spiritual life remained unsatisfied. Jesus entered her life. He recognized her faith in Him, cleansed her of sin, and gave her new hope. 'Emma' needed this as much as every other person on earth. Jesus satisfied her need for real life, real love, and fulfilling relationships by giving her Himself. He does the same for you. No matter what you've done and who won't forgive you, Jesus does—through faith in Him!

We don't just need a teacher. We need a Savior who comes in and does for us what we can't do for ourselves: forgiveness. All of our debt before God is enormous; we are incapable of ever paying it back.

Read Hebrews 10:22.

What does God promise that He will do for your conscience when you draw near to His presence by faith?

Dwell on the FACT that Jesus will cleanse your conscience from guilt. Will you take Him at His word? If there is any past sin for which you are still feeling guilty, claim God's complete forgiveness today. You can simply tell God,

"Thank You for forgiving me, thank You for cleansing me...Thank You for being bigger than my sins, and being able to turn things around in ways I cannot imagine. With Jesus' help, I receive the assurance that You have forgiven me. Help my heart catch up with my head on this. Help me to see that You allowed me to go down that dark path into sin because You are able to redeem even the worst things we do." (Sue Bohlen, Probe Ministries, Sept. 2012)

Now, choose to believe you are forgiven and allow Jesus to cleanse your conscience from any residual guilt. Every time you think about it again, thank God for His amazing gift!

JESUS SATISFIES YOUR HEART WITH FORGIVENESS

Recommended: Listen to the podcast "Immoral Woman: Jesus Satisfies Your Heart with Forgiveness." *Use the following as a listener guide.*

Like the woman washing Jesus' feet with her tears in Luke 7, many of us carry the guilt of our sins with us like a heavy burden, weighing us down. The continual reminder of our sins keeps us from experiencing freedom and from enjoying the relationship with God that we have by faith in Jesus Christ. You and I need to understand how complete and continual is God's forgiveness of us. And, we need to know how to deal with any recognized sin in our lives so that we won't carry that guilt.

Sin is any violation of the moral character of God or the law of God. We sin by thinking evil, speaking evil, acting evil or omitting good. Whether we like this description or not, sin is a rebellion in our hearts against God as our authority. Without forgiveness for our sin, we are separated from God.

In the Bible, the term "forgiveness" means "to send off or send away." Our sin is transferred to a substitute, Jesus, and taken away. People in Old Testament times were accepted by God and received eternal life in the same way as we do today: by faith in the merciful grace of God. For daily living, however, they had to bring their animal sacrifice to the priest. Their sins were transferred to that sacrifice, and they received forgiveness for their sins up to that point. In Luke 7, Jesus declared forgiveness of sins to a sorrowful, sinful woman without a sacrifice, shocking the other guests. He did this because of her faith in the merciful grace of God.

God promised His people that one day forgiveness would no longer be a temporary solution, but be complete and permanent. That happened on the cross through Jesus.

As Paul declared in Colossians 2,

> *"When you were dead in your sins...God made you alive with Christ. He forgave us **all** our sins, having canceled the charge of our legal indebtedness, which stood against us and*

*condemned us; He has **taken it away**, nailing it to the cross."* (Colossians 2:13-14)

Once you place your faith in Jesus Christ, whatever you have done that was wrong in God's eyes from the time you were born through the time of your death has been canceled. Taken away. All of it. Past, present and future. Nailed to the cross.

It's even better than that. As 2 Corinthians 5:19 says,

> *"that God was reconciling the world to Himself in Christ, not counting people's sins against them."*

Since your sins have been taken away, God is longer counting them against you. Just like the woman in our lesson today, you are forgiven based on your faith alone. Sins are applied to Jesus who takes them on your behalf. Once you have trusted in Jesus, Ephesians 1 says that forgiveness is something **we possess as believers**. We receive God's forgiveness for all our sins (past, present, and future) from the moment we place our faith in Jesus Christ. That is very important for you to know. Forgiveness is complete and continual.

Although our God does not hold our sin against us any longer, and His grace is continually forgiving us of sin, that does not give us permission to intentionally sin. Intentional sin does not fit with who you are as a forgiven Christian with a new life to enjoy.

But, as long as we live in these earthly bodies, we will be tempted to sin. Sin will happen—whether intentionally or unintentionally. So, as an already forgiven Christian, you might ask, "How do I deal with sin when I recognize it in my life?"

Great question. Here's the biblical process for dealing with sin as a believer:

Step One: View yourself rightly.

Your identity is not "_____" (coveter, greedy, gossiper, whatever that sin is).

> You are in Christ, a child of God, who sometimes "_____" (covets, is greedy, gossips).

Step Two: Recognize (confess) the truth regarding your sin.

To **confess** biblically means *to agree with God about what you and He both know to be true*. Confession is not a formula, a process, or dependent on a mediator. Regarding sin in my life, it is not saying, "I'm sorry." It is saying, "I agree with you, God. I blew it!" You see your sin as something awful!

> *Using sexual immorality as an example: while reading 1 Thessalonians 4:1-8, the Spirit convicts you that sexual immorality in any form is not pleasing to God. You are instructed to "flee/avoid immorality." You recognize this sin in your life. You agree with God that your immoral sexual behavior is seeking love and acceptance from the wrong source. It doesn't fit someone who knows God. That is confession.*

Step Three: Confession is incomplete without repentance.

Repentance means *to change your mind about that sin, to turn away from it, to mourn its ugliness, resulting in changing your actions.* Paul says that godly sorrow brings repentance (2 Corinthians 7:9-11). Like the woman in Luke 7. It's saying, "I recognize what I am doing is wrong. This fills me with sorrow because it hurts You, God. Please help me to live differently." That's how our lives get transformed.

> *For sexual immorality: You want to live in order to please God, and God wants you to avoid sexual immorality. So, you pray, "Lord Jesus, please have your Spirit nudge me when I am not holy and honorable with my body. Help me to say no to temptation and to give up any relationship that is not honorable to you. By faith, Lord, I want you to do that in my life." That is repentance.*

Repentance requires that you change something. You can confess "until the cows come home" (daily, habitually) and never change anything. Jesus called for people to "repent" not "confess."

Step Four: Repentance leads to dependence.

Depend on the living Christ inside you for that change to take place. Our Lord Jesus Christ is not interested in our compliance (outward conformity) as much as He desires our **obedience from the heart.** Dependence on God leads to obedience.

> *For sexual immorality: Memorize 1 Thessalonians 4:1-8 and any other scriptures that deal with staying pure and not rejecting God's instructions. Be sensitive to the Spirit's nudging when you are tempted to do otherwise. Choose to live a life that pleases God.*

Our God created us with a spiritual thirst for a relationship with Him. Another human cannot satisfy that thirst. Only God can satisfy the thirsty heart. The complete and continual forgiveness we receive by faith in Jesus satisfies our thirst for love and acceptance. This forgiveness motivates us to live a life that pleases Him. As the Bible promises,

> "for He satisfies the thirsty and fills the hungry with good things." (Psalm 107:9)

A satisfied heart basks in forgiveness, love and acceptance.

Let Jesus satisfy your heart with the goodness of His love.

Reflect

Is there any ugliness in your life that you mourn? Follow the steps above to live in freedom from that ugliness. Will you trust Jesus to work on this area of your life?

For example, if you are currently in immoral behavior, such as an affair, pornography, living with or attracted to someone who is not your spouse, what choices do you need to make in order to flee from immorality or leave your life of sin? Be confident that your Heavenly Father has given you everything you need in order to do this.

Pray: Ask Jesus to satisfy your heart through knowing Him. Trust Him to work in your life to bring you healing, hope, and freedom. Thank Him for His grace toward you and His unending love for you.

Deeper Discoveries: Read Luke chapters 9-12. Reflect on what you read.

Luke 9—

Luke 10—

Luke 11—

Luke 12—

♡ 4 Two Women Needing HOPE

"He said to her, 'Daughter, your faith has healed you. Go in peace and be freed from your suffering.'" (Mark 5:34)

> Pray: Lord Jesus, please teach me through this lesson.

A Little Bit of History

Hopefully in our study so far, you have seen how absolutely different the Lord Jesus Christ was from His culture in the way He regarded women! Thus, as Jesus' ministry unfolded, the average citizen of Israel began to witness an extraordinary approach to women, one that cut against the grain of commonly held practices. Jesus treated women as no man had ever treated them before. His warmth, personal attention, tenderness, sound teaching, and compassion toward women were revolutionary.

Jesus taught God's Word to large crowds in the area around Capernaum on the north shore of the Sea of Galilee. As He taught, He also healed many people who were in desperate need of hope in their lives. The news about His teaching and the miracles spread, drawing large crowds wherever Jesus went. One day in the midst of one of these large crowds, Jesus encountered a woman and a girl who were also in desperate need of hope.

Read Mark 5:21-24.

Where was Jesus heading and why?

Read Mark 5:24-29.

Focusing on the Sick Woman

Let's call the woman 'Dottie.'

From verses 25-26, describe 'Dottie' and her circumstances.

Her condition is probably uterine hemorrhaging like a number of women experience with endometriosis or fibroid tumors. Some of the medical treatments available for her condition included carrying ashes of ostrich eggs on your body and taking ground-up willow bark—a bitter-tasting remedy containing salicin, an aspirin-like drug, that would have only aggravated her bleeding. According to the Mosaic Law, anyone with this condition was considered unclean until healed. She was excluded from the temple area (and synagogue seating), excluded from mingling with others, and considered separated from God. Anyone who touched her or anything she touched would be unclean. Dottie needed hope for a different kind of life.

Think about the kind of life 'Dottie' had led for 12 years. Considering what you as a woman enjoy in life, what did she miss out on?

What brought 'Dottie' to Jesus for healing (verse 27)?

The prevailing opinions of her day were that bad things didn't happen to good people. The thought was that everyone got what they justly deserved. Thus, to be stricken with a chronic, incurable disease such as this was equated with sinful behavior, presumably being immoral. People shunned her. She was not invited to parties, weddings, or to anyone's house for dinner. She couldn't even sit in the women's section of the synagogue. If married, her husband would be unclean for 7 days after every sexual encounter with her; perhaps she had been divorced and shut off from her family. She is an outcast—lonely, isolated, and probably in a state of clinical depression.

No one brought her to Jesus. But, she heard about Him and acted on that news. It's our job to share with others about how Jesus can change lives. No one knows how many times it takes for someone to pay attention and respond. All we can do is tell.

Put yourself in her shoes. As an ordinary woman, what emotions would 'Dottie' have experienced...

- As she reached out to touch Jesus' cloak (verses 27-28)?

- After she felt healing (verse 29)?

Read Mark 5:30-34.

After Jesus willingly extended His healing power to 'Dottie,' what did He do next (verses 30-32)?

What did 'Dottie' do then (verse 33)? See also Luke 8:47.

Then, what did Jesus say to her (verse 34)?

When Jesus insisted that she publicly reveal herself, how would that be an advantage to her?

Two Women Needing Hope 47

'Dottie' acts on her own faith—mixed with some superstition about His garments ("If I just touch His clothes"). Later it was a common practice for the crowds to touch the hem of His garments and be healed. Here Jesus chooses to single out this woman's case for clarification. There is no magic in the garments of Jesus. Even if there is superstition in the woman's mind, Jesus honors her faith, "I will be healed" (verse 28).

Jesus knew what happened because He was always God. He laid aside His glory and did not use His attributes for Himself while on earth. But He always knew what those around Him were thinking before they spoke. It is a dramatic moment for Jesus and for the fearful woman. When she revealed herself and told what she did and why, Jesus affectionately called her "daughter," signifying a relationship with Him (and possibly a clue to her age), and publicly declared her healed. She was now freed from her suffering.

Jesus sent the healed woman off in peace to a changed life of wholeness and hope. She could enter society because she was healed AND she received spiritual life as well. Our God always does more than we ask or think!

Focusing on the Girl (and Her Family)

Reread Mark 5:21-23.

The local synagogue was the place of worship and instruction in the community. Worshipers gathered once a week to pray and read the Scriptures. Services included prescribed readings, prayer, and a sermon. Respected teachers who were visiting for the Sabbath were usually invited to speak.

The **ruler of the synagogue** was a layman whose responsibilities included such things as looking after the building (maintenance, repairs, and cleaning) as well as supervising the worship (conducting services, selecting participants and maintaining order). He sat in the reserved seats for elders and rulers and was a very important man in the community.

Since Jesus called the girl 'Talitha' (verse 41), that's what we will call her, too.

What do you learn about 'Talitha?' See also Luke 8:41-42.

What did Jairus want Jesus to do (verse 23)?

The synagogue ruler was a prominent and usually wealthy man. But he had a problem that neither his prominence nor his wealth could solve. His precious daughter was dying. Jairus is very specific in what He wants Jesus to do. "Come and touch her." The Jews believed that the touch transmitted vitality. Jairus had faith in Jesus' touch, and he expressed that faith. Jesus acts upon the faith we have which is wonderful and encouraging to us. But, would Jesus take time out to go to Jairus' house for a little girl? The answer is, "Yes." To Him, this little girl is just as important as anyone else. He starts off with the crowd following Him.

Read Mark 5:35-43.

During the interruption when Jesus healed 'Dottie,' what has now occurred at Jairus' house (verse 35)?

What does Jesus tell Jairus in verse 36? See also Luke 8:50.

Jesus heads to the house and sees a commotion—mourners at work, weeping and wailing. Paid mourners developed as a profession in Old Testament times and continued into the time of Jesus. As a career that passed from mother to daughter, professional mourners were almost always women. Their mourning included loud wailing, sad songs, and eulogies, sometimes accompanied by flutes.

What does Jesus say to the wailing crowd outside Jairus' house (verse 39)?

What was the wailers' response to Jesus?

Who went into the room with Jesus (verses 37 & 40)?

Once inside, what did Jesus do then (verses 41-43)? (Notice His tenderness toward the girl through His words and gestures.)

How is Jairus' initial faith challenged and stretched through this whole incident?

Reread Luke 8:50. What was Jesus' plan all along?

After hearing that his daughter was dead, Jesus told Jairus to stop being afraid and to keep on believing for she would be healed. Since being afraid and believing are mutually exclusive, you can't do both at the same time. The Psalmist writes, *"I will trust and not be afraid."* (Psalm 56:3) It's as though Jesus was saying to Jairus, "I'm still on it."

This is important for us as well. When fear overwhelms us, we can with an act of our will stop being afraid and choose to believe God that He is "on it" and will not abandon us. Fear is an emotion; faith is an act of the will. From Jairus' viewpoint, he had to wait an agonizingly long time for Jesus to respond to his request through delays, diversions, and disappointing news. Jesus had not forgotten Jairus. He could have healed the girl from a distance, but He didn't. He stretched Jairus' faith through the waiting.

Faith is learning to say to Jesus, "Lord, I can't do this on my own. But, You can do this in and through me. I will trust You." Then, see what He does.

BEING SATISFIED BY HIS LOVE

Jesus stopped His public ministry to heal two women—one publicly; the other privately. One was socially dead; the other was physically dead. One touched Him and was healed without a word; the other He touched and spoke to when she was healed. One was an outcast; the other was loved within her family circle. Both received the hope of new life.

Two women were beyond human help and without hope. 'Dottie' was held in bondage to her disease and could not have a proper relationship with her God or her community. Jesus lovingly took notice of both of them and gave them hope through healing. Jesus took time away from the crowd to minister to each one personally. He used endearing terms ("daughter" and "little girl") to address them, not just "woman" and "child." He satisfied their immediate needs and gave them abundant life and hope for the future.

Jesus also gave 'Dottie' an opportunity to tell her story publicly. Her pain caused her to seek help from Jesus by faith. Everyone hears her tell *why* she touched Him and *how* she had been instantly healed.

> *Describe any of your own painful, hopeless circumstances that have driven you to Jesus. What did you learn about His faithfulness through that experience? How did others minister to you in love, showing Jesus to you and giving you hope?*

JESUS SATISFIES YOUR HEART WITH HOPE

Recommended: *Listen to the podcast <u>"Two Sick Women: Jesus Satisfies Your Heart with Hope."</u> Use the following as a listener guide.*

In the crowd pressing around Jesus is a woman with a desperate need. Her life is a living death, and her condition is hopeless. Having suffered for 12 years with no break, she is likely pale, emaciated, and weakened. She used all her financial resources to seek out one doctor after another, yet she was worse. This desperate woman hears about Jesus. Hope flickers in her heart.

Sadly, no friend has brought her to Jesus. She acts on her own faith—mixed with some superstition about His garments. She reaches out and touches His cloak. Immediately, her bleeding stops. She feels it. She knows she is completely healed. It is a vivid moment of joy for her!

As Jesus took time out from His busy schedule to minister to two women personally, He also takes a personal interest in each one of us. Yet, as He meets our individual needs, Jesus has the right to choose what He brings into our lives. He wants us to stop being afraid and to keep on believing, to exercise the faith that we have. All of this offers hope to anyone going through what seems to be insurmountable odds.

What is hope?

The kind of hope that the world offers is generally the wishful thinking kind where someone is not sure they will get what they want or need but "hopes" they will.

Biblical hope is the confident expectation that God will fulfill His promises to you because it is based on the character and faithfulness of God.

You need hope when you are facing something tough, when you are sad, or when you can't see the end of a painful time. Losing hope leads to discouragement and despair. Hope is essential to human life. In Titus 2, Jesus is called "our blessed hope," promising that Jesus is coming back to earth to make right whatever is wrong. But, in the meantime,

Jesus offers us hope now. In the midst of troubles, He satisfies our hearts with hope through healing and through comfort.

Hope through healing

Let's talk first about hope through healing. The psalmist said this,

> "Praise the Lord, O my soul, and forget not all His benefits—who forgives all your sins and heals all your diseases." (Psalm 103:2-3)

As we learned in the last lesson, once you trust in Jesus, all your sins—past, present, and future—are completely forgiven. You don't have to wait on that. But what about the "heals all your diseases" part? We know through experience that God doesn't automatically heal every Christian from every disease. You or someone you love dearly may be struggling with a chronic illness or a debilitating injury. And when you read through the gospels, seeing Jesus heal so many people instantly, it's easy to question why that doesn't seem to be true today.

So, let's look at two things: why Jesus performed so many miracles and how He heals today.

1. Why did Jesus perform so many miracles?

Miracles authenticate the message and the messenger. Jesus' miracles demonstrated that He is God and that His message, therefore, has authority (Acts 2:22).

Miracles also demonstrate God's compassion for His people. Through His miracles, Jesus showed that...

> - **He has power beyond that of an ordinary man.** The laws of the natural world, which He created, were not boundaries for Him.
>
> - **He is the fulfillment of prophecy concerning the Messiah.** The Messiah would be recognized by the works He would do—healing the blind, freeing prisoners, and releasing the oppressed. Jesus basically said to people "I am that one."
>
> - **He is God on earth.** In John 6:25, Jesus calls miracles "signs," pointing to the fact that He was the Messiah—God on Earth. The crowds just wanted the benefits—food, protection, health. Jesus wanted people to believe that He was their God in human form.

2. How does God still heal today?

God still performs miracles today though we may not see them as often as we'd like. Miracles still authenticate the message and the messenger. For someone claiming to do miraculous things, always make sure their message exalts Jesus as the **only** way to God, that the Bible is their **only** authority, and that forgiveness of sins is found **only** through Jesus Christ. Then, you can be confident that you are seeing the genuine works of God. Remember that the greatest miracle is what God does to change a human heart from the inside out and redeem a lost life. He is doing that in abundance.

In Psalm 103, the phrase "heals all your diseases" could also refer to God enabling the human body to heal itself. God created the human body with a marvelous immune system. Yet, you've no doubt seen where the same treatment for a disease will work well for one person but not for another. We don't understand why. But, we must trust God's goodness in what He chooses to do.

Jesus has the right to choose what He brings into our lives. He tells us to stop being afraid and to keep on believing, to exercise the faith that we have, and to hold onto hope.

When God withholds or delays healing, He promises comfort.

Hope through comfort when healing is delayed

Paul writes in 2 Corinthians,

> "Praise be to the God and Father of our Lord Jesus Christ, the Father of compassion and the God of all comfort, who comforts us in all our troubles, so that we can comfort those in any trouble with the comfort we ourselves receive from God. For just as we share abundantly in the sufferings of Christ, so also our comfort abounds through Christ." (2 Corinthians 1:3-5)

The promise is that Jesus comforts us in ALL our troubles. That includes those that just seem to happen to us like chronic illness or pain as well as those we cause because of wrong choices we make. Paul had a chronic physical illness. He writes about it in 2 Corinthians,

> "Three times I pleaded with the Lord to take it away from me. But He said to me, 'My grace is sufficient for you, for my power is made perfect in weakness.' Therefore I will boast all the more gladly about my weaknesses, so that Christ's power may rest on me. That is why, for Christ's sake, I delight in

weaknesses, in insults, in hardships, in persecutions, in difficulties. For when I am weak, then I am strong." (2 Corinthians 12:8-10).

God loved Paul dearly; he was doing the work God gave him to do. But, God's answer was still, "No." So, Paul said, "I will boast in my weakness so that Christ's power may rest on me." That frees us and moves us in the direction that will give us hope.

Through any life challenge, including physical debilitation, God wants us to learn to not depend on ourselves but to depend on God and His great power. He wants us to put our hope in Him and count on His work to deliver us when we are in the midst of troubles. Sometimes we want to just quit. It's God's power in us that makes us strong during those times. In His strength, we receive hope through comfort.

Even the most loving parents must let their children hurt (cutting teeth, riding a bike) sometimes in order for them to live as adults. God loves you more than the best parents can and wants you to learn how to live as His child, depending on Him for the comfort and strength that flows from His grace to you.

Human parents raise their children to be less dependent on them and more independent. But, God raises His children to be less independent and more dependent on Him. Whatever He brings into our lives that makes us more dependent upon Him is good for us.

You may feel that God isn't noticing your pain. He knows. He chooses what will make you more like the Lord Jesus Christ. And suffering is an important instrument in His hands much as you may hate it.

In your pain, say to Him, *"I am your daughter, Lord. Help me to deal with this situation. Please give me your hope and comfort."* Remember that God is good all the time. You can trust His goodness in whatever He chooses to do in your life. Trouble is part of human life. Christians who are loved by God will suffer some troubles in this world, but **Jesus is Your comforter** when you hurt.

Our God created us with a spiritual thirst for a relationship with Him. Another human cannot satisfy that thirst. Only God can satisfy the thirsty heart. Jesus Christ satisfies our thirst for hope and comfort when we need it. As the Bible promises,

"for He satisfies the thirsty and fills the hungry with good things." (Psalm 107:9)

A satisfied heart faces any dire situation with hope.

Let Jesus satisfy your heart with the goodness of His love.

Reflect

> What in your life right now is very tough, sad, or otherwise painful? Believe that God loves you even though He allows you to go through that pain. Ask Jesus to heal your diseases. And, while waiting, ask Him to fill your heart with comfort and hope as you endure pain and suffering.

> Often God uses our Christian brothers and sisters to share Jesus' comfort with us. With whom have you shared your pain? Have you allowed them to pray for you? To assist you? To give you comfort?

Pray: Ask Jesus to satisfy your heart through knowing Him. Trust Him to work in your life to bring you healing, hope, and freedom. Thank Him for His grace toward you and His unending love for you.

Deeper Discoveries: Read Luke chapters 13-16. Reflect on what you read.

Luke 13—

Luke 14—

Luke 15—

Luke 16 —

5. A Woman Needing FREEDOM

"Mary Magdalene went to the disciples with the news: 'I have seen the Lord!' And she told them that He had said these things to her." (John 20:18)

> Pray: Lord Jesus, please teach me through this lesson.

A Little Bit of History

As Jesus continued His public ministry, more and more people began to travel with Him from one town to the next. Some were no doubt just curious onlookers. But others followed because they wanted to accompany the person who had so radically changed their lives. Mary, the Magdalene, was one of those.

Mary came from Magdala, a small village on the western shore of the Sea of Galilee, southwest of Capernaum. Once famous for its fine woolens and dyed products (the dye coming from shellfish caught in its waters), Magdala had as many as 4,000 inhabitants with 80 weavers' shops. It was also known by two other names—Magadan and Dalmanutha. In Jesus' day, it was primarily a Gentile city with a lot of Roman influence. Two gospel writers record Jesus going there (Matthew 15:39-16:4; Mark 8:10-12). Perhaps that is when He met the woman we now know as Mary Magdalene.

A WOMAN NEEDING FREEDOM 59

Read Luke 8:1-3.

List every reference to women, including names and any information given about them.

Mary Magdalene had been freed from the bondage of demons (also called evil or unclean spirits) controlling her life. Demon possession was exhibited in a variety of ways—blindness, deafness, muteness, seizures, irrational behavior, crippling of body, cutting oneself, and/or violent behavior. Anyone who was in such spiritual bondage lived a miserable existence. There is no scriptural evidence that Mary had been immoral. A church leader around 500 AD associated Mary with the immoral woman in the previous passage (Luke 7:36-50), but there is nothing in the biblical text to support that.

How might being a demon-possessed woman have affected Mary's life...

What did these women do as they followed Jesus (verse 3)?

Consider the activities that "helping to support them" as He traveled might have involved. List as many as you can.

Jesus did not use daily miracles to provide for His own needs and for those of His 12 disciples as He traveled throughout Galilee and onward to Jerusalem 70 miles away. Instead, He lived as a man daily dependent upon God to provide. In this way, He could identify with all of humanity and gave opportunity for men and women to support His ministry. This set an example for later apostles and missionaries to be supported by those who benefited from their preaching. These women probably gathered and prepared food, washed clothes, filled water jars, repaired clothing and sandals, baked bread, and perhaps paid for shelter at an inn.

Based upon what you have learned so far, how did Jesus' acceptance of what these women did for Him go contrary to the culture?

Why do you think these women supported Jesus by their service and their money?

How did traveling with Jesus also benefit them?

Jesus accepted their money and their service as an act of worship, love and gratitude. Other rabbis might have taken the money in an offering but never accepted their close presence. These women were blessed by just being with Him and hearing His teaching over and over again. They saw every miracle. They watched Him interact with people—alongside the 12 disciples. They were unofficial disciples who became a part of the early church.

Read Matthew 17:22-23 and Luke 24:6-8.

What information did Jesus give to His disciples (and the women) to prepare them for the future?

So, when Jesus headed to Jerusalem for the Passover, Mary Magdalene experienced firsthand the events of the last week of Jesus' life. Consider the joy and expectation she probably felt during His triumphal entry and His cleansing of the Temple. Yes! But, she may have felt anxiety about what would happen in Jerusalem. Then, she experienced the agony and horror of His arrest and trial. What a shock!

Read Matthew 27:55-61.

How did Mary Magdalene and the other women continue to minister to Jesus at His crucifixion?

Read Luke 23:55-24:1.

After His death, what did Mary Magdalene and the other women do to continue their ministry to Jesus?

At a time when most of Jesus' 12 disciples deserted Him (except for John), these women stayed close to Him. In this case, being "lowly women" (in their culture) was an advantage because they weren't seen as a threat.

Read Matthew 28:1-10 and answer the following questions.

Who saw the angels? See also Mark 16:1, 5-6 and Luke 24:1 & 10.

What did the angel(s) tell the women to do (Matthew 28:5-7)?

Who saw Jesus (Matthew 28:8-9)?

How did they respond to Jesus (Matthew 28:9)?

What did Jesus tell the women to do (Matthew 28:10)?

Read John 20:1-9.

John only mentioned Mary Magdalene's presence at the tomb. We know from the other gospels that Mary was not alone at the tomb (verse 2, "we"). Perhaps she left to tell the disciples after the angel's announcement in Matthew 28:1-7. Like John, let's focus on Mary's experience on that beautiful morning.

When Mary Magdalene ran to the disciples, what was her concern (verse 2)?

Read John 20:10-18.

After the disciples left, what did Mary do and see (verse 11-12)?

When asked by the angels why she was crying, what is still her concern (verse 13)?

When she turned around, whom did she see (verse 14)?

When asked by Jesus why she was crying and whom she was looking for, what does her response (verse 15) reveal about her boldness as a woman?

What happens when Jesus calls her by name (verse 16)?

Faithful Mary went to the tomb, ready to prepare Jesus' body properly, probably thinking this was her last opportunity to serve Him. When she saw the empty tomb, she felt helpless to find Him and to care for His body. Three times she wants to know where He has "been put." She wants to find Him and declares, "I will get Him." How could she do that? This is such a bold statement from one gutsy woman!

Jesus calls her by name, and she recognizes Him. Mary may have embraced Jesus physically (as did the women in Matthew 28:9-10) for the Lord responded, "Do not hold onto Me, for I have not yet returned to my Father."

What responsibility does Jesus give to her (verse 17)?

How does Mary respond (verse 18)?

Because of a twisted interpretation of the Mosaic law, the rabbinical leaders taught that women were uneducable. They were also considered unreliable as courtroom witnesses. Even the disciples didn't believe their words at first (Luke 24:11). Yet, God entrusted these women to be reliable witnesses for Him. The women faithfully told the disciples that Jesus was alive.

Why do you think God entrusted the spectacular news of the resurrection to women?

"That a woman would be the first to see Him is an evidence of Jesus' love as well as a mark of the narrative's historicity. No Jewish author in the ancient world would have invented a story with a woman as the first witness to this most important event." (Walvoord and Zuck, *The Bible Knowledge Commentary New Testament*, p. 342)

SATISFIED BY HIS LOVE

Mary Magdalene was once held in spiritual bondage. She experienced misery. Perhaps she was shunned. Her family may have been burdened to care for her. Then, Jesus came into her life and gave her freedom. Out of gratitude and love, she freely chose to travel with Jesus and care for His needs with money, effort and time. Mary followed Jesus to Jerusalem and was present at the cross.

Jesus satisfied her immediate need for freedom from bondage and gave her abundant life. Jesus intentionally taught everyone who followed Him, including women, what it means to know, follow, depend upon, and obey Him. And, those who had been forgiven and healed wanted to give back to the One who had set them free from their pain.

In what ways do you give back to the One who has set you free? How do you support Jesus today?

JESUS SATISFIES YOUR HEART WITH FREEDOM

Recommended: Listen to the podcast "Mary Magdalene: Jesus Satisfies Your Heart with Freedom." *Use the following as a listener guide.*

In the story *The Count of Monte Cristo*, Edmun Dantes escaping from a cruel captivity lands on a beach occupied by smugglers who force him to fight a man named Jacabo to the death. When Dantes has the chance to kill his opponent, he spares his life and plants the knife into the sandy beach instead. Jacabo's immediate response is, "I am your man forever"—implying today, tomorrow and the next day—not knowing what would be ahead for him, grateful for his freedom.

Considering what Dantes did for Jacabo, Jesus did that and more for us. He set us free! And, out of gratitude, each of us should choose to serve the very One who did it. Not knowing everything ahead of us, we can declare, "Lord Jesus, I am YOUR woman"—today, tomorrow, and the next day. But, what would that look like?

To be set free means that you are in bondage to something. We've already seen how Jesus frees you from bondage to lies by giving you truth in Himself and in God's Word. He frees you from sinfulness by giving you complete forgiveness and a restored relationship with God. Jesus frees you from bondage to chronic illness by offering you hope that He is going to get you through it, right by your side.

Jesus freed Mary Magdalene from her spiritual bondage to demons. Because of your faith in Jesus you are also freed from spiritual bondage because a greater power moves into your spirit—the Holy Spirit Himself. He sets you free from the power of sin and Satan to become what God intended you to be.

But, there is another kind of spiritual bondage—that of expectations based on outward performance. Maybe you started out accepting the gift of salvation by faith in Jesus as a free gift. But then you have been thrown into a works-related way of living this Christian life in order to maintain your acceptance before God. The Bible calls this "living by law." That's bondage.

Living by law can be any man-made system of works by which people attempt to approach God on their own merits or performance. I'm not talking about what is clearly taught in the New Testament about living a life that pleases God. Sin is still "sin." I am talking about those extra rules that some person or organization devised for you to follow to be a "good Christian" and for God to love you. Such extra rules could include: how often you must go to church, which church you must attend, what kind of clothing you must wear, and things you must do or say every day to stay in God's good favor. The result is that you stray from enjoying a love-based relationship with Jesus to practicing a religion. When you are living this way, your spiritual life is in bondage to feelings of obligation, guilt, and fear of punishment for not doing it right.

Jesus wants to set you free from that. Living by grace rather than living by law is freedom. The Bible says in Ephesians 2,

> "For it is by grace you have been saved, through faith—and this is not from yourselves, it is the gift of God—**not by works**, so that no one can boast." (Ephesians 2:8-9)

Here's the key truth that will set you free from any bondage to religious performance: by grace are you saved. Grace means "undeserved favor." It's a gift that neither you nor anyone else deserves. God gives His favor to someone not because they are good enough to deserve it but because **His love chooses to do so**. We all receive this grace when we trust in Jesus.

God wants you to relate to Him now on the basis of **His grace**. Jesus paid the complete price for you to be set free from your sinful past. You can do nothing more to make yourself acceptable to God. Paul understood those who had been relating to God through outward performance. For years, he had been there! He writes how God's abundant grace changed his life when he says this,

> "Even though I was once a blasphemer and a persecutor and a violent man, I was shown mercy because I acted in ignorance and unbelief. The grace of our Lord was poured out on me abundantly, along with the faith and love that are in Christ Jesus." (1 Timothy 1:13-14)

Out of God's mercy comes His grace to you. God's grace is so abundant it's like a cup overflowing. This overflowing grace sets you free from whatever has you in bondage—sin, guilt, religious expectations, whatever. Paul was describing himself, but doesn't it also describe Mary Magdalene? It also describes you.

God's grace is His undeserved favor abundantly poured out on those who desperately need Him. You and I desperately need Him.

His grace overflows to you every single day. You are completely forgiven and covered in God's grace—His gift to you of love and acceptance in His eyes. Who would say "no" to that?

Paul writes in Romans 6 that we *have died* with Christ and are raised with Him to a new life. This new life has a new identity—*you are in Christ, a child of God, totally forgiven, accepted and loved by God.* That's who you are from the moment you placed your faith in Jesus Christ and how God sees you! This new identity SETS YOU FREE to live a radically different life. You're dead to the old "you" and alive to the new "you" in Jesus.

So, how do you respond to God's grace that has freed you from spiritual bondage and gives you a chance to live a new life? You respond with love and gratitude for what Christ has done. You respond to God's grace by saying,

> "I love you, Lord. I thank you, Lord. I want to approach life your way rather than my own way. I am YOUR woman, Lord, ready to serve you."

That's what Mary Magdalene did. She responded to His grace. She was willing to love Him, obey Him, and serve Him with her life. She responds out of love and gratitude, not out of obligation.

Grace motivates you to serve Jesus out of love and gratitude for what He has done for you. You want to live the kind of life that pleases God because you love Him and are thankful for what He has done for you. You can freely accept Jesus' complete payment for your every sin (past, present and future) on that cross and your new identity—you are in Christ, a child of God, one of His saints, totally forgiven, accepted and loved by God. You can freely say, **"Lord Jesus, I am YOUR woman"**—today, tomorrow, and the next day. You can freely make that choice to serve Him wholeheartedly, without obligation or fear.

God wants you to relate to Him on the basis of His grace, so that your obedience is based on His love for you, your love for Him, and gratitude for what Christ has done for you. Relax! You have been set free from whatever spiritual bondage you have experienced. Thank Him for this wonderful FREEDOM!

You plead my cause, you right my wrongs
You break my chains, you overcome
You gave Your life to give me mine
You say that I am free, how can it be
(Lauren Daigle, How Can It Be)

Our God created us with a spiritual thirst for a relationship with Him. A relationship with another human cannot satisfy that thirst. Only God can satisfy the thirsty heart. As the Bible promises,

> "for He satisfies the thirsty and fills the hungry with good things." (Psalm 107:9)

A satisfied heart will want to say, "Lord Jesus, I am YOUR woman—today, tomorrow, and forever."

Let Jesus satisfy your heart with the goodness of His love.

Reflect

> *How have you been relating to God through outward performance, such as religious works or good deeds, with the accompanying feelings of obligation, guilt, and fear of punishment for not doing it right? Recognize that you have been set free from that by God's grace through your faith in Jesus Christ. Will you let His grace to you motivate you from this day forward to love Him, obey Him, and declare, "Lord Jesus, I am Your woman?"*

Pray: Ask Jesus to satisfy your heart through knowing Him. Trust Him to work in your life to bring you healing, hope, and freedom. Thank Him for His grace toward you and His unending love for you.

Deeper Discoveries: Read Luke chapters 17-20. Reflect on what you read.

Luke 17—

Luke 18—

Luke 19—

Luke 20—

6. Two Women Needing ASSURANCE OF LOVE

"Jesus loved Martha and her sister and Lazarus. So when He heard that Lazarus was sick, He stayed where He was two more days." (John 11:5-6)

> Pray: Lord Jesus, please teach me through this lesson.

A Little Bit of History

After two years of ministering in Galilee, Jesus returned to Judea and Perea, territories near Jerusalem, to minister there. In Jerusalem, He healed a man by the Pool of Siloam and told a parable about Himself as the Good Shepherd who would give His life for His sheep. Somewhere in Judea, He answered the question, "Who is my neighbor?" with a parable about a good-hearted Samaritan who helped a fellow traveler. After that, He went to Bethany.

Bethany was a small village on the southeastern slopes of the Mount of Olives about two miles east of Jerusalem on the Jericho Road. It still exists today. Martha, Mary, Lazarus and "Simon the leper" lived there. The Mount of Olives, from which Jesus could see Jerusalem, is about 2 miles long and has three peaks. The modern road from Jericho to Jerusalem still passes along its southern slopes. Rising about 100 feet above Jerusalem, it gives an unforgettable view of the city, which is to the west.

Read Luke 10:38-42.

Upon seeing Jesus and His companions in her village, Martha opened her home to Him (verse 38)—hospitality in action for quite a large group of men.

As manager of the home, what might have been Martha's initial emotions and thoughts (verse 38)?

Look at Martha's attitude change as time progresses. What became Martha's focus, and what does she do (verse 40)? [Consider what is involved in hosting that size of a crowd.]

Toward whom was Martha's anger directed and why (verse 40)?

Where was Mary's focus at this moment (verse 39)?

In Jesus' response to Martha, what was His focus (verses 41-42)?

Martha opened her home to Jesus and His disciples. This was a large group, understandably requiring quite a bit of preparation to feed and house them. Then, Martha gets distracted from her welcoming attitude and literally "stepped up to and burst upon" Jesus in her frustration. In her anger at her sister Mary, she makes a demand of Jesus. In His love, Jesus confronted Martha with her wrong priorities. His focus was on this opportunity for both she and Mary to learn from Him. She needed to let go what was distracting her (and others) from that.

Read John 11:1-6.

Mary and Martha sent word to Jesus that Lazarus was ill, yet they did not ask Him to come to Bethany though they probably expected it (John 11:21,32).

Knowing the need, what did Jesus decide to do (verse 6)?

Two days later, Jesus makes the announcement that they would go to Bethany.

Read John 11:17-27.

How did Martha respond to the news that Jesus was near (verse 20)?

As each woman came to Jesus, you will notice that both speak the same words of confidence in Him (Martha in verse 21, Mary in verse 32). Both sisters already knew that Jesus had brought two people back from the dead (Mark 5; Luke 7). But, neither of those had been laid in a tomb yet. Both were confident in His power. But, Martha went a step further and expressed that she knew Jesus could do something about it even now.

What does Jesus declare to Martha?

- Verse 23—

- Verses 25-26—

How do Martha's answers reveal that she had also been listening to Jesus' teaching?

- Verse 24—

- Verse 27—

Martha's confession of faith is similar to Peter's in Matthew 16:16. In fact, what Martha says is even more amazing because she makes her declaration with her brother dead now for four days, already in the grave! Her response to Jesus' question, "Do you believe this?" is a firm, "Yes, Lord." The emphasis in the original language is that this is her firm and settled faith.

Read John 11:28-37.

When Martha called her sister Mary, what did she do (verses 29 and 32)?

When Jesus saw Mary and the people around her weeping, how did He respond (verses 33-35)?

What does this tell you about Him?

John 11:35 is the shortest verse in the Bible, yet it conveys to us so much about the love of Jesus. Jesus wept; He shed tears. He identified with us as humans so much that He could express deep human sympathy from His heart with Martha and Mary. Sorrow had touched those close to Him. As you have already read in John 11:4 and 23, Jesus planned from the first hearing of the news to let Lazarus die then to restore his life to him. Their present hurt would soon be healed.

Read John 11:38-46.

Because of Palestine's warm climate, burial usually took place the same day as death. Friends and other family members prepared the body for burial by washing the body and clipping the hair and nails. Strips of linen were then wrapped around the body. Spices (hyssop, rose oil, aloe, and myrrh) were placed between these strips. Placing a linen napkin over the face, the body was laid on an open bier and carried to the tomb—usually a natural cave or a tomb cut into a rock. A large round stone was then rolled across the entrance of the tomb after burial thus sealing it. After the flesh had decayed and only the skeleton remained, the bones were put into a small box called an ossuary, which was then placed on a shelf carved out of the tomb wall. In this way, a whole family could be buried in the same tomb.

After Jesus tells the people to remove the stone, what is Martha's objection (verse 39)?

How does Jesus respond to her in verse 40? Do you think He knows her pretty well by now?

Describe the scene in verses 43-44 as though you were there watching it. [It's okay to picture Jesus smiling as He greets Lazarus.]

Jesus stated His mission for this situation:

> "for God's glory so that God's Son may be glorified through it" (John 11:4)
> "that they may believe that you sent me" (John 11:41-42).

According to verse 45, what were the results?

After the raising of Lazarus, Jesus made His departure. But, after a short stay in Ephraim (15 miles away), He returned to Bethany to stay for His last days. On Sunday, Jesus entered Jerusalem triumphantly, riding on a donkey. On Monday, He pronounced a curse on a barren fig tree and drove out the merchants and moneychangers from the Temple. On Tuesday, He answered a question about paying taxes to Caesar and pointed out a widow giving her small coins in the Temple. That evening, He taught His disciples on the Mount of Olives. Then He went to a dinner with His friends in Bethany, at the home of Simon whose life had also been changed. Four people whose lives are undeniably touched and changed by Jesus gratefully honored Him…

Read John 12:1-11.

By the time of this dinner, Jesus had been in Bethany for 4 days.

How did each of the sisters show their gratitude to Jesus for giving life back to their brother (verses 2-3)?

- Martha —

- Mary —

Do you think Jesus knows Mary pretty well by now?

Not everyone was as pleased with Mary's gift. But, Jesus recognized it and responded to their pettiness.

Read Mark 14:6-9.

How did Jesus come to Mary's rescue?

What do you think Jesus meant by saying, "she did what she could" (verse 8, NIV)?

Martha worshiped Jesus through serving Him and His disciples without complaining. Mary worshiped Jesus through giving her most precious possession. Mary perceived with her delicate woman's intuition what the apostles failed to understand though repeatedly and plainly told to them by Jesus—His impending execution. Jesus accepted Mary's act of worship and said that Mary did what she as a woman in her culture with her resources could do for Him. He called that "a beautiful thing to Me" (NIV).

In what ways could Jesus say, "she did what she could" about you (in your life circumstances) when it comes to showing gratitude to Him?

SATISFIED BY HIS LOVE

When Jesus met Mary and Martha, they needed neither healing nor a cleaned-up reputation. Yet, they still needed assurance of His love for them. His love didn't allow Martha to stay focused on the wrong things (tasks & choices) so He confronted that and gave new direction. His love defended Mary when she was criticized by His own disciples. His love gave her respect and commendation instead. His love allowed both of them to learn from Him. When Lazarus died, Jesus assured them of His love by going to be with the sisters and then raising their brother back to life. He accepted their different ways of thanking Him. Mary and

Martha could serve Him, love Him, and worship Him in different ways—all equally as valuable.

Jesus understood their different personalities and behavioral tendencies. He understands that about you as well, quirks and all. He knows how to love you and how to lead you. Think about your tendencies to control a situation or not, how quickly you shed tears or not, or how you speak before you think. He knows you well and still loves you dearly. He hurts when you hurt and rejoices when you rejoice. He knows how to respond to **your** needs, which will be personally applied and different from how He responds to your "sister's" needs. He knows how to love you well.

> *Are you okay with that? Or, are you still telling Him how He should do things, telling Him how He should be God?*

> *Reread John 11:39-40. If Martha insisted on having her own way, what would she have missed? Apply Jesus' answer to Martha to your own expectations from Him. How will you let Him lead you in the right direction for you?*

JESUS SATISFIES YOUR HEART WITH ASSURANCE OF HIS LOVE

Recommended: Listen to the podcast *"Mary & Martha: Jesus Satisfies Your Heart with Assurance of His Love."* Use the following as a listener guide.

Jesus and His disciples often stayed in Bethany when they were near Jerusalem, probably with Martha, Mary, and Lazarus. Jesus knew His friends' home was a place of welcome, protection, rest, and provision. Martha and her siblings knew the joy of Jesus' private company and His love.

Mary and Martha were not suffering from illness, demonic possession, or sinful reputation when Jesus first met them. They apparently were not destitute, needing Him to provide for them. But, believing that Jesus could be the promised Messiah, they still needed and wanted a relationship with Him. Remember this...

> "Even people with incredible character are not born again until they meet and trust in Jesus." (Vivian Mabuni, IF:Gathering 2017)

Jesus' love in action

Over time, Martha and Mary received assurance of His love for them. His love didn't allow Martha to stay focused on the wrong things so He stopped her bad thinking and redirected her toward what was truly important. His love protected Mary from unwarranted accusation from her sister and from His own disciples. When their brother died, Jesus' love compelled Him to travel to be with them and to cry with them. His love promised them hope, then fulfilled that promise. Jesus, as fully God and fully man, truly loved them.

The Bible teaches that God so loved the world that He gave His only Son so anyone could believe in Him and receive eternal life (John 3:16). You are part of the world that God loves. And, once you accept His gift of eternal life through your faith in His Son, you get even more of God's love for you.

Jesus said in John 16,

> *"the Father God Himself loves you because you have loved me and have believed that I came from God." (John 16:27)*

He loves you!

Paul wrote this in Romans 5,

> *"God has poured out His love into our hearts by the Holy Spirit, whom He has given us." (Romans 5:5)*

As a believer in Jesus, you will have the assurance that your God loves you. He pours out His love into your heart so you can experience that love. You can count on this truth—**God loves you**.

But, love isn't soft. Love doesn't always make it easy on the one loved. Jesus didn't make it easy on Martha and Mary and Lazarus. In John 11:3, Martha informed Jesus that Lazarus, "the one you love is sick." John 11:5 says that, "Jesus loved Martha and her sister and Lazarus." That is plainly stated. They knew He loved them. All 3 of them.

Jesus knew what was going on in their lives. Lazarus was deathly ill and soon died (verses 6, 11, 14). And, Jesus let it happen. Jesus could have done something about it. Martha was confident in His **love** for them and in His **power** to heal. Jesus could have healed Lazarus from a distance the moment He received the news as He had done several times before this (for example, Mark 7:24-30 and John 4:46-53). Yet, He didn't.

Jesus chose to do something different, even better than what anyone could imagine though it caused pain and suffering to those He loved and a lot of waiting, too (John 11:14-15). Instead, He allowed these friends whom He loved dearly to endure pain and suffering for several days because there was a greater **good** they could not see at the time. Jesus loved them and hurt right along with them.

After 4 days of being dead, Lazarus was brought back to life, and good things happened. God's goodness showed up—Lazarus had his life restored, his sisters saw their now healthy brother returned to them, the disciples witnessed an amazing work of God, and many people now believed in Jesus who had not yet believed in Him.

Martha could now say to herself with assurance, **"Jesus loves me. Jesus knows what is going on in my life. Jesus can do something about it. I can trust His goodness in whatever He chooses to do."** And, so can you.

Assurance of His Love in your Life

How confident are you that Jesus loves you? Do you need assurance that He loves you?

You are loved by your God. Love is good because God is good. And, God's love for you is unending. I am convinced of this. God wants you to know this:

> *"For I am convinced that neither death nor life, neither angels nor demons, neither the present nor the future, nor any powers, neither height nor depth, nor anything else in all creation, will be able to separate us from the love of God that is in Christ Jesus our Lord." (Romans 8:38-39)*

Nothing. Not you, not anyone or anything, can separate you from God's love for you because you have believed in Jesus. Jesus loves you consistently, constantly, and completely. Be assured of this.

If you think that you are suffering because you've done something wrong to make God stop loving you—that's a lie! Erase it from the "auto-fill" workings of your mind. Replace it with these four truths you can count on:

1. Jesus loves you.
2. Jesus knows what is going on in your life.
3. Jesus can do something about it.
4. You can trust His goodness in whatever He chooses to do.

He may not bring back your dead loved one or heal your sickness or make everything right. But, His goodness and love will choose to do whatever is best for you, for others, and for God's glory.

Our God created us with a spiritual thirst for a relationship with Him. A relationship with another human cannot satisfy that thirst. Only God can satisfy the thirsty heart. As the Bible promises,

> *"for He satisfies the thirsty and fills the hungry with good things." (Psalm 107:9)*

A satisfied heart can go forward with complete assurance that your God knows how to love you well!

Let Jesus satisfy your heart with the goodness of His love!

Reflect

Read the following song lyrics.

Higher than the mountains that I face
Stronger than the power of the grave
Constant through the trial and the change
One thing remains, this one thing remains
Your love never fails, and never gives up;
It never runs out on me
Your love

Because on and on and on and on it goes
Before it overwhelms and **satisfies my soul**
And I never, ever, have to be afraid
One thing remains, this one thing remains
Your love never fails, and never gives up; it never runs out on me
Your love

(One Thing Remains by Jesus Culture)

Now write the four truths below to etch them in your mind. Make them personal, "Jesus loves me..."

Pray: Ask Jesus to satisfy your heart through knowing Him. Trust Him to work in your life to bring you healing, hope, and freedom. Thank Him for His grace toward you and His unending love for you.

Deeper Discoveries: Read Luke chapters 21-24. Reflect on what you read.

Luke 21—

Luke 22—

Luke 23—

Luke 24—

> Keep reading to preview Lesson One of the next study in this series, *Seek the Treasure*. This is a short and easy study of the book of Ephesians.

Preview of "Seek the Treasure"

Discovering what it is and how to find it through Ephesians

1: The Treasure of Jesus Christ

"That power is the same as the mighty strength [God] exerted when He raised Christ from the dead and seated Him at His right hand in the heavenly realms, far above all rule and authority, power and dominion, and every name that is invoked, not only in the present age but also in the one to come." (Ephesians 1:19-21)

> Pray: Lord Jesus, please teach me through this lesson.

THE ABC'S OF EPHESIANS—AUTHOR, BACKGROUND, AND CONTEXT

Like any book you read, it always helps to know a bit about the author, the background setting for the story, and where the book fits into a series (its context). The same is true of Bible books.

AUTHOR

A man named Paul authored the letter we know as Ephesians. He lived at the same time as Jesus and for many years afterwards. But, we have no indication that he ever met Jesus before the Resurrection. Paul was a well-educated, devout Jew. Jews believed in the one true God and followed the Mosaic Law, which was God's law for them.

At first, Paul didn't believe Jesus was the Son of God and fought against Christians, dragging them out of their homes and putting them in prison. He was determined to wipe out all the Christians. Then, one day, Jesus appeared to him and grabbed his attention. After believing in Jesus Christ as his Savior, Paul was sent by Jesus to take the gospel to the people who were not Jews, called Gentiles in the Bible.

In the Bible, he is known by two names: his Hebrew name "Saul" and his Roman name "Paul." To keep things simple, we will call him by his Roman name because that's what he mainly used in his travels and ministry.

Paul took "missionary journeys" to many cities in the Roman Empire. Wherever Paul and his co-workers visited, people heard the message about Jesus and became Christians. The new believers met together and formed a church in that city. Paul loved those people very much and wanted to hear how the young churches were doing. Someone would bring him news about the church members in a particular city. Then, Paul would write them a letter, usually answering some questions they had or teaching them something they needed to know about living as Christians.

The Holy Spirit guided Paul to write those letters and preserved 13 of them for us to have in our Bibles. In fact, Paul authored more of the New Testament writings than anyone else. These letters are a gift to us 2000 years later.

Background

On his third missionary journey, Paul went to the large city of Ephesus. The Ephesians were obsessed with power, especially the use of magic. They were very afraid of evil spirits and bad luck so they clung to anything that would keep them safe. That included magic words written on socks or recited aloud to chase evil spirits away, necklaces with magic power to give them luck when playing sports, and books of magic spells to use for protection. So, Paul spent three years with the Ephesians, teaching classes every day to those who wanted to learn a new way to live. Many became Christians and gave up their old way of life.

A few years later, on a visit to Jerusalem, Paul was falsely accused and arrested. After a long time of waiting to be released, he finally appealed to Caesar and was sent to Rome. That's where Paul was when he wrote this letter—imprisoned in Rome, chained to a Roman soldier 24/7. But, he was given the freedom to have visitors and write letters, including this letter to the Ephesians.

The letter to the Ephesians was written about 4-5 years after Paul left Ephesus. Before his arrest, Paul had met briefly with the Ephesian church leaders in a nearby city to give them words of encouragement. He received news about the church from various sources. But, he had not been back to Ephesus.

Context

The letter to the Ephesians is one of four letters Paul wrote from his Roman imprisonment that the Holy Spirit chose to preserve in our New Testaments. The others are the letters to the Philippians in northern

Greece, to the Colossians in central Turkey, and to Philemon who was a leader in the Colossian church.

The order in which we find Paul's letters in the New Testament is not based on chronology but mostly on size. Ephesians is found after Galatians which was written more than 10 years earlier. Philippians and Colossians follow. But, Philemon, the shortest letter, is found at the end of Paul's letters.

Ephesus and Its treasure Chest

Two words described Ephesus—prominent and obsessed. The city was prominent because of its location along major highways, its commercial prosperity, and its large population of ¼ million people. It also had impressive buildings, including the Roman governor's office.

Ephesians were obsessed with the supernatural, especially the power of evil spirits that could make their lives miserable. The city was filled with magicians, psychics, and astrologers. The people tried anything that would defeat the enemy and guarantee a "successful" life.

Prominent and obsessed are both related to power. For the Ephesians, life was all about power. Who or what had the most power? And, their identity came from their power sources. That was reflected in their treasure chests.

God's Treasure for Them and for Us

Paul taught the Ephesians that Jesus Christ was the Son of God who came to earth to live as a human, died for their sins, and was resurrected from the dead to give them new life. Paul's message everywhere was consistently the same. "Believe in the Lord Jesus Christ, and you will be saved."

Paul started as usual in the synagogue preaching to Jews and interested Gentiles. Some of the synagogue leaders put a stop to that. So, Paul took the new Christians with him and began daily teaching sessions in a local lecture hall for the next two years. The book of Acts describes this time.

Read Acts 19:8-12.

> *How effective and far-reaching was Paul's teaching in Ephesus (verse 10)?*

The Ephesians' concept of power was that of an impersonal substance one could use to one's own advantage. What did God do through Paul to get their attention on Him instead (verses 11-12)?

Miracles are already amazing, but God did more than usual. The Greek word translated "extraordinary" means "to hit the mark like one who is throwing a javelin or arrow." God was targeting their need for spiritual power with "extra-miraculous" miracles. God showed them that He was **more powerful** than their magicians, lucky charms, and magic words. God was more powerful than the evil spirits or any substitute they might trust for protection against evil. God knew what they really needed—Himself!

Our very creative God knows how to use His power to target your spiritual need as well. How has God targeted your need and drawn you closer to Him?

Read Acts 19:13-20.

Invoking names to control evil spirits was a form of magic practiced in Ephesus. The practice had been taken up even by Jews.

When the news about the magicians who tried to imitate Paul became known, what happened (verse 17)?

What did the new believers in Christ do (verses 18-19)?

What was the result (verse 20)?

Many Ephesians trusted in Jesus for their protection, so they got rid of their substitutes. They had a big bonfire to burn their sorcerer's manuals, lucky socks, and magic necklaces. They attended Paul's classes then spread out and shared the good news about Jesus throughout western Turkey, establishing churches all over the place. The letter to the Ephesians was written to the church in Ephesus and to the churches in the surrounding area. The Holy Spirit guided the writing of this letter so it is a gift from God to us. Let's dig into it.

Read Ephesians 1:1-2.

As mentioned in the ABC's of Ephesians, Paul wrote this letter to the Christians living in Ephesus.

Read Ephesians 3:1 and 8.

What does Paul say about himself (verse 1)?

What was his mission from God (verse 8)?

Paul knew he was a prisoner of Rome, but he considered himself a prisoner of Christ in whom he had entrusted his life.

THE POWER OF JESUS CHRIST

As you study Ephesians, you will see that Paul reminded them, and us, that no matter how hard life gets, Jesus Christ is still more powerful than any substitute "good luck charm." And, Christ's power makes it possible for us to live God's way today and not be afraid.

Let's find out how powerful Christ is and how His power works for us.

Read Ephesians 1:19-23.

> *In verses 19-20, what does Paul want the Ephesians to know about the might of God's power?*

> *Where is Christ (verse 20?*

> *Over what does He have authority (verse 21)?*

> *Over what else does He have authority (verse 22)?*

What is meant by "all rule and authority, power and dominion" in verse 21? That phrase includes all spiritual powers—the good angels, the demons, and Satan himself. We've mentioned evil spirits in this lesson so far, but we really haven't answered the question, "Who are they?"

Evil spirits are demons. They are angels created at the beginning of creation. The Bible teaches that one angel rebelled against God and took 1/3 of the angels with him. We know that rebel leader as Satan, also called "the devil," and those with him in rebellion against God as "demons." Satan and his demonic forces do everything they can to thwart the good purposes of God—gaining control over people through deception, counterfeits, fear, manipulation, and torment.

In His life on earth, Jesus as the Son of God demonstrated that He had greater power over all the spirit world—the good angels who served Him plus Satan and his demonic forces. The resurrected Jesus, in heaven once again, is still more powerful than Satan and any demon. Jesus Christ has the power of a great king who is king above all other powers and kings.

"Every title that can be given" refers to those names used in magical formulas to control evil spirits as you saw in Acts 19:13. Demons were behind every reference to evil spirits.

Read Ephesians 2:6.

Where does God place us as believers?

In the mind and plan of God, all Christians are seated with Christ in heaven under His powerful authority. Notice that we are not under Christ's feet like all the angelic powers. We are seated within His authority over anything that could come against us.

People in our western culture don't consciously admit to being afraid of evil spirits like the Ephesians were and like some parts of our world still are. But, we do fear bad things happening and try to manage supernatural power in such a way that results are "virtually guaranteed" in our favor. As a culture, and really as humans everywhere, we seek anything that will satisfy the spiritual hunger in our souls and "guarantee" successful living.

WHAT ARE YOUR SUBSTITUTE POWERS?

Do you possess anything that you think gives you good luck—a pair of socks, a special shirt, a rabbit's foot? Why do you think that item has power to give you good luck?

Some things are associated with causing bad luck—walking under a ladder, breaking a mirror, stepping on sidewalk cracks, or jinxing a pitcher throwing a no-hitter.

But, do you think those things really have power to give you or others bad luck?

Those are substitute treasures. The most powerful treasure we could ever have is Jesus Christ. We have no need for any substitutes to keep bad things from happening to us. We don't need lucky socks, magic words, or special charms to make sure good things happen to us. Substitute treasure is worthless.

YOUR TREASURE IN CHRIST

What do you tend to rely upon in order to be "successful" in life or to defeat any perceived "enemies?" Self-sufficiency? Academic degree? Social status? What else?

Are you willing to learn how to get rid of your substitutes and cling to your treasure in Christ alone?

Through Paul's message to the Ephesians, our God is saying to you and me, "Why trust in any substitute power to help you live a good life?" Nothing is as powerful as Jesus Christ Himself. His power is available to every believer through His Spirit living inside you.

Christ wants you to get rid of those substitutes in your head as well as in your heart and your experiences. You can say to Him, *"My treasure in you, Lord Jesus, is more powerful and valuable than anything I could substitute for You. Please confirm that in my heart."* Will you do that today?

Get *Seek the Treasure* at melanienewton.com as well as most online bookstores. Also available on Kindle.

Sources

The following resources were used in the preparation and writing of this study.

1. *The NIV Study Bible New International Version,* Zondervan Bible Publishers, 1985.
2. Vickie Kraft teaching notes on New Testament women
3. *Nelson's Illustrated Bible Dictionary*
4. *New Unger's Bible Dictionary*
5. Sue Bohlin, "Christianity: The Best Thing That Ever Happened to Women," www.probe.org
6. Vivian Mabuni, *IF:Gathering 2017*
7. Carol Kent, *Becoming a Woman of Influence*